CORRECTIVE CAPITALISM

The Rise of America's Community Development Corporations

Neal R. Peirce and Carol F. Steinbach

Photographs by Shepard Sherbell

FORD FOUNDATION • NEW YORK

A complete list of Ford Foundation
publications may be obtained from the
Foundation, Office of Reports, 320 East
43 Street, New York, N.Y. 10017.

Library of Congress Cataloging-in-Publication Data

Peirce, Neal R.
  Corrective capitalism.

  "A report to the Ford Foundation."
  1. Community development, Urban — United States.
2. Community development corporations — United States.
I. Steinbach, Carol. II. Title.

HN9O.C6P45   1987   307.7'6'0973   87-15040
ISBN 0-916584-28-3

457 July 1987

CONTENTS

4

Early in 1986 Neal Peirce and Carol Steinbach, both experienced economic and political observers, were asked by the Ford Foundation to undertake a daunting assignment: to survey the universe of community development corporations (CDCs) throughout the United States, to trace their evolution over the past two decades, and to show how they connect to some of the difficult social and economic challenges of our times. The authors looked not only at urban CDCs but also at the growing number of community organizations that are attacking similar problems in rural America.

There are now community-based institutions working to revitalize distressed city neighborhoods and rural communities all across the United States. Few of them existed a quarter of a century ago. They vary considerably in size, scope, and funding sources, but virtually all share certain basic characteristics: they operate within a geographically defined low-income target area; they are controlled by the people who live in that area; and they undertake housing and economic development projects in addition to providing such social services as job training, credit unions, and day-care and senior centers. CDCs finance and operate shopping centers, industrial parks, business "incubators," and retail franchises. They also act as advocates in pressing city hall for better municipal services and in challenging banks to increase their lending in poor neighborhoods.

The Ford Foundation has played a continuing role in the genesis and evolution of the community development movement. During the early 1960s the Foundation's Gray Areas program, which provided grants to organizations in several cities, foreshadowed the federally financed anti-poverty initiatives that were to follow. In the mid-1960s the Foundation began supporting several first-generation CDCs, spread geographically from Brooklyn to the Mississippi Delta to Los Angeles. The aim was to build a type of local development institution that would avoid the shortcomings of some of the earlier efforts and give priority to social and economic programs that would produce visible improvements in poverty areas.

By the mid-1980s the Foundation's involvement in community development had grown to include major support of local and national financial intermediaries as well as direct funding of emerging CDCs in two dozen cities. Our total investments thus far amount to some $170 million. These funds have supplemented other, larger resources, which in the early years came principally from the federal government. When federal support for community development began to dwindle in the 1980s, CDCs were obliged to broaden their funding and streamline their operations. As the authors note, CDCs have forged alliances and partnerships with a wide assortment of funders, including local governments, states, churches, foundations, banks, private corporations, and, in some cases, universities and hospitals. In the process, many CDCs have become sophisticated entrepreneurs of development and have achieved more economic and civic influence than anyone would have thought possible a decade ago.

Peirce and Steinbach have traced this evolution, interviewing scores of CDC managers and community residents, as well as staff from Ford and other foundations, state and local government officials, and business leaders who have been sympathetic supporters of the movement. They talked with skeptics as well. They were given complete freedom to describe and make judgments on what they saw and heard.

As their report makes abundantly clear, we have in the CDC a model that works in revitalizing low-income communities. But here I would echo the word of caution sounded by many of those interviewed by Peirce and Steinbach. Despite the considerable good that has flowed from the "new localism," in fact no substantial development among the poorest communities and people is achievable without an adequate flow of public resources. Nor is it realistic to believe that the current revenue bases of state and local governments will be sufficient to compensate for the lack of federal funding. Given the amounts and types of subsidies required in most community development projects, there is just no substitute for the federal presence.

Peirce and Steinbach have produced a compelling document, one that describes the CDC movement both in personal terms and in the context of the larger forces that have been at work. Their story is a positive one, of people working against considerable odds to bring new life and opportunity to their communities. We owe them a debt of gratitude for reminding us of the creativity and resiliency of the human spirit.

Franklin A. Thomas
President
Ford Foundation

The South Bronx, long a symbol of urban deterioration, still has mean streets like this one, but others are being revived through the efforts of several community development corporations.

INTRODUCTION

It's a blustery winter day in the South Bronx, N.Y., 1977. It looks like Berlin in 1945 — so many gutted buildings, smoldering fires, or the fresh ashes of those recently extinguished. This day, in a tiny hole-in-the-wall luncheonette, Megan Charlop is talking. Megan is a young woman who once thought of becoming a lawyer, worked in the city courts, and decided the only hope for the South Bronx was in the neighborhoods. Now, whenever she hears a landlord has abandoned an apartment building, she goes in, calls the tenants together, and tells them: "You have two options. You can stick together, pool your rents, and work with the city and with us to get this building into shape. Or you can all sit here and freeze, one by one." This winter, she has helped save seventeen South Bronx tenement buildings.

Megan Charlop works — often seven days a week, for meager pay — for the Peoples' Development Corporation, one of scores of community development groups that have sprung up in seemingly hopeless New York neighborhoods. The groups work in the midst of abandoned, gutted, burned-out buildings, garbage-strewn alleys, drugs and crime. It is a time when building abandonment runs rampant in the South Bronx, when a prominent member of the *New York Times* editorial board is urging euthanasia for such neighborhoods — cutting off city services and letting those areas die as a part of a strategy of "planned shrinkage" of the city.

But the Megan Charlops are throwing their lives into the battle on the other side. And the results are sometimes incredible. When residents of endangered buildings or neighborhoods realize they can make decisions for themselves, attitudes and habits change abruptly. Crime, vandalism, and drug usage plummet. Buildings that police once feared to enter become self-policing.

The community development movement of the United States has had its moments of national recognition, as for example, when Robert Kennedy paved the way for the Bedford-Stuyvesant Restoration Corporation in Brooklyn, N.Y. back in the 1960s. But mostly the movement has developed and matured as quietly as Megan Charlop going from building to building in the winter of the South Bronx's deepest discontent. From a handful of pioneer community development corporations (CDCs), it has spread into nearly every state, into cities large and small and remote rural areas. There is no precise count; estimates range between 3,000 and 5,000 CDCs in the mid-1980s.

In a decade of contracting federal domestic activity, CDCs along with their allies in churches and other nonprofit organizations, have become the principal suppliers of low-income housing in the United States. CDCs finance and operate shopping centers, industrial parks, business "incubators," and retail franchises. They start their own businesses; increasingly, they provide venture capital, loans, and technical assistance to other job-producing enterprises. Their social service arms, from health to child care to drug counseling to care of the elderly and homeless, mediate between individuals in need and a society that provides cold and bureaucratic services, if any.

For many Americans the mention of "community organization" conjures up 1960s images of radicals storming city hall, of civil rights marches, anti-Vietnam protests, lettuce boycotts, and distrust of anyone in a business suit. In fact, many of today's successful CDCs had their roots in that period. But with rare exceptions, the 1960s are now as much history for them as for the rest of American society. One can't very well hurl his body into the path of an oncoming bulldozer when he (or she) is the developer. Community development organizations today are becoming increasingly sophisticated, drawing support from a growing number of state and local governments, and from an ever-widening universe of private foundations and corporations. Slowly, the beginnings of an urgently needed infrastructure of "intermediary" support agencies is emerging — groups such as the Local Initiatives Support Corporation, which since 1980 has raised more than $130 million for community economic development projects, or the Development Training Institute, which has trained more than 150 CDC leaders.

The directors of today's community development organizations are savvy and well-schooled in deal making. Many have worked in the private sector or in government. Some have advanced business or law degrees. Quite a few grew up in the neighborhoods they are now trying to revive. They manifest a special quality that one private lawyer who helps CDCs described as "confident arrogance." Many would succeed, one mayor told us, at running even the largest private corporations.

As with any institution, CDCs should be eyed with healthy skepticism. CDCs and their supporters sometimes romanticize the movement's effectiveness. But there are instances enough of "dream" projects and neighborhood jobs that failed to materialize. Some CDCs are inefficient, poorly managed, plagued by internal tensions, inert, occasionally — though rarely — corrupt. There remain too few states and communities in which governors, mayors, and private-sector leaders understand how CDCs can be integrated into comprehensive economic and human development. For every community or needy neighborhood with an effective CDC, there are a dozen without.

But this movement, largely invisible to the society at large, is quintessentially American. It mirrors the qualities of our society that so impressed Alexis de Tocqueville in the 1830s: our penchant for innovative civic association, our belief that individuals can bring about change, our openness to risk taking and to bridging lines of class, ideology, and party. CDCs, in their quiet way, have become a major component of corrective capitalism; in this free-enterprise nation they are finding ways to open doors to classes and individuals otherwise excluded from the American dream.

In January of 1986 the Ford Foundation asked us to write a report for the general public on the condition and dynamics of the community development movement in America. With the encouragement of Ghebre Selassie Mehreteab, the Foundation's program officer dealing with many of the newly created CDCs and intermediaries of the 1980s, we surveyed the scene in cities and rural areas across the country, visiting CDCs of all varieties — large, small, "mature," and "emerging." Many of the groups had been funded by Ford, many had not. We talked with founders and fervid backers of CDCs, including some of the movement's "fathers," as well as skeptics out in the field. We met with leaders from foundations, state and local government, and business. We were given total editorial freedom.

Our inherent thesis is that America's government and private leaders should elevate CDCs to a central position in domestic policy making. The problems of the American poor and underclass, which CDCs seek straightforwardly to address, have confounded traditional liberal and conservative formulas. Neither heavy government spending on the one hand, nor supply-side economics on the other, has "solved" problems that lie deep in community and social disorganization. CDCs have learned to prosper on the rocky soil of even the poorest neighborhoods; each of their successes is a small miracle, and a contribution to the greater society. CDCs are no longer a theoretical, untested model. From their roots in the 1960s, they have grown and flourished over a quarter of a century.

Neal R. Peirce
Carol F. Steinbach

Children playing in North Philadelphia. Once dangerous and desolate, the neighborhood now surprises the visitor with solar town houses, rehabilitated apartment buildings, community gardens, and new stores.

CHAPTER ONE

Diamonds in the Rough

From the war in Vietnam to the war on poverty — Sam Smith was in for a shock when he returned to North Philadelphia in 1969 after military duty in Southeast Asia. The neighborhoods he'd known as a boy were in shambles. Scores of refuse-strewn empty lots had been left by urban renewal's bulldozers. The grand old black entertainment street of Columbia Avenue was in a downward spiral triggered by the riots following Martin Luther King's assassination in 1968. Homeowners refused to spend money on their property, expecting to be displaced as nearby Temple University bought up land for potential expansion.

Seventeen years after his return from Vietnam, Sam Smith drives visitors through North Philadelphia. One would have to be callous beyond belief not to be overwhelmed by the crumbling mortar and graffiti, deep poverty and abandonment. The North Philadelphia ghetto is no single pocket of decay. Stretching block after block, it covers a vast expanse of one of America's great cities.

But North Philadelphia is not without its surprises. Suddenly Smith is showing off twenty-three new solar town houses. Pointing to 200 other units of new or rehabilitated housing. Noting some 400 parcels, taken by the city for nonpayment of taxes and now "land banked" for future projects. Talking about community gardens, a thrift store, the start of commercial rehabilitation along Columbia Avenue. And taking visitors to a new trash recycling plant that has created a handful of jobs for hard-core jobless youth plus a source of income for scavenger trash collectors.

A CDC, the National Temple Non-Profit Corporation, Sam Smith its president, is sparking this development. Begun in 1968 by congregants of the National Temple Baptist Church, it has a rich agenda, ranging from community advocacy to real estate management, block-captain organization to town watch, free food for the hungry (18,000 meals annually) to technical assistance for small businesses.

National Temple is no stranger to failure: not all the projects it has dreamed up have obtained funding. But confidence in this CDC's capacity to deliver has risen so sharply in Philadelphia that in 1986 it received $550,000 for operations, another $1.5 million for projects. Among the multiple sources: Community Development Block Grants, city appropriations, the Catholic Church's Campaign for Human Development, CIGNA, American Express, the Local Initiatives Support Corporation, the Ford Foundation, Pew Memorial Trust, the Mellon Bank.

What manner of organization tackles the toughest societal problems, plays charity and capitalist and community organizer at the same time, and can manage to bring government, corporate, philanthropic, religious America all on board?

The answer is the community development corporation. CDCs vary dramatically in their origins, their track records, their styles, their wealth, the types of urban and rural communities they serve. Not all even call themselves CDCs, using instead such varied designations as "neighborhood development organizations" or "economic development corporations." About 99 percent are nonprofit, most often tax-exempt "501(C)3" organizations, which makes it easier to attract foundation and government grants. Commonly, CDCs spin off for-profit arms to do development work or operate profit-making enterprises.

The universe of nonprofit organizations serving the poor is vast, ranging from traditional social service organizations such as United Way to groups with more of a development focus — a category that includes CDCs as well as cooperatives, minority business development programs, and neighborhood housing services. There are no "neat" lines. But the following three characteristics are present in the National Temple Non-Profit Corporation and in fact in all CDCs.

Community control. CDCs sprang out of the neighborhoods, starting in the 1960s when the notion that community residents could define and control development in their communities was considered radical. Twenty-five years and thousands of new CDCs later, this is one element of the "experiment" that is widely regarded as an unqualified success. Control by boards of directors composed primarily of community residents is a virtually immutable constant.

National Temple's fifteen-person board is not untypical. In addition to neighborhood residents, it includes representatives from CIGNA, Bell of Pennsylvania, and the Philadelphia Urban Coalition.

A few CDC boards play a limited, passive, or largely ceremonial role. But that is rare. Most boards are far more active, with members making important contributions to fund raising, community relations, lobbying, and credibility building. In many CDCs, board members also play a major role in setting policy and choosing projects; in some, board members are involved in actual project implementation.

Quite a few CDCs have created subsidiary boards or special advisory committees composed of local business and political leaders. The granddaddy of CDCs, Brooklyn, N.Y.'s Bedford-Stuyvesant Restoration Corporation, pioneered this approach. Its operational arm, the Restoration Corporation, administers overall CDC operations under the directorship of a local board. A companion organization, the Development and Services Corporation, contributes business contacts and expertise. Its directors over the years have included such corporate and political leaders as former Treasury Secretary C. Douglas Dillon, former Senators Jacob Javits and Robert Kennedy, CBS chief William S. Paley, Chemical Bank Vice Chairman Richard K. LeBlond, and business magnate Benno C. Schmidt, Sr.

It's not unknown for debilitating fights to break out among CDC board members or between boards and staff. Some tensions, it would seem, are almost inevitable. But by and large, relations are harmonious.

Economic development. Every CDC undertakes economic development projects. Most are of a "hard" development character — constructing or rehabilitating housing and commercial real estate, starting businesses, creating jobs for local residents. Most CDCs also have a "softer" component more directly related to human services — child care and elder care, skills training, home-ownership counseling, summer camps, health screening, drug and alcohol abuse programs, for example. Whatever the development mix, the goal of every CDC is the immediate relief of severe economic, social, and physical distress — and, eventually, wider regeneration of the community.

Targeting. All CDCs focus their activities in a clearly defined geographic area encompassing a high concentration of low-income people. This may mean a heavily disadvantaged, underclass urban neighborhood such as North Philadelphia, the South Bronx, or Watts in Los Angeles, where CDCs strive to rebuild dilapidated housing, to rekindle a spark of economic vitality, to reverse residents' overwhelming sense of negativism and isolation, and to send a signal to the community outside that the decline has "bottomed out."

Other CDCs focus on trying to stem decline in ailing working-class neighborhoods in danger of further deterioration. Quite often the chosen method is to combine "hard" development with CDC-sponsored programs to promote stabilization through home ownership. Consider the Northeast Denver Housing Center, in a single-family residential neighborhood, roughly two-thirds black, an area interspersed with commercial strips populated by liquor stores, fast-food outlets, pawn shops, and bars. Twelve neighborhood groups started the Housing Center in 1982. They prevailed on John Stovall, retired after thirty years' civilian service with the Air Force, to serve as director.

Stovall — black, businesslike, indefatigable — scraped up subsidies from the city and state governments, the Piton Foundation (Denver's prime funder of neighborhood-based projects), local banks, and later the Ford

Foundation. By 1987, the Housing Center had provided counseling to more than 1,500 first-time home buyers, including information on how to get a mortgage or remove a blot from one's credit rating. It had assisted 600 homeowners behind on mortgage payments and in danger of foreclosure, negotiating with banks and helping some residents obtain small tide-over loans from the city's housing agency. Through its buyer incubation program, the Housing Center had instructed tenants in its own units on how to raise a down payment and care for their own homes. And it had bought fifty-eight HUD- and VA-foreclosed houses and readied them for low-income purchasers.

An alternative CDC focus may be to try to restore vitality to deteriorating shopping and commercial strips. A prime example: East Liberty Development Inc. (ELDI) in Pittsburgh. The city prevailed on the local Chamber of Commerce to start ELDI in 1979. But the real spark for this CDC came from an aggressive branch manager of the Mellon bank, who dragooned East Liberty business, church, and civic leaders into his basement for a decisive meeting on how the new CDC could begin turning things around. The challenge was formidable. East Liberty's array of once-thriving neighborhood stores and retail chains had been steadily hemorrhaging, down from 242 establishments in 1963 to only 98 in 1977. A grand $68 million city-sponsored urban renewal "experiment" in the 1960s — erecting traffic barriers to turn East Liberty into an area of pedestrian shopping malls — had backfired, repelling the neighborhood's working-class clientele, and making it virtually impossible for the heavy flow of downtown commuters to get to East Liberty stores.

With major financial support provided by the city, the Ford Foundation, the Howard Heinz Endowment, and the Mellon Bank Foundation, ELDI launched an aggressive campaign to lure businesses back to East Liberty. Its approach: a combination of hard-nosed promotion tactics and hands-on business assistance, targeted to large developers and small enterprises alike. ELDI services range from writing business plans and packaging financing to help with advertising, site selection, job training and recruitment, even exporting goods abroad. By 1987, 120 new businesses had opened in the neighborhood, creating 1,200 jobs. Four major new private developments were completed or under way — two new shopping centers, the conversion of an abandoned warehouse into loft-style condominiums, the rehab of an old department store. The city resurfaced major roads and tore down the traffic barriers. East Liberty businesses reported their best sales months ever in 1986.

Some CDCs concentrate on restoring and preserving housing for poor people in neighborhoods undergoing middle-class "gentrification." In Richmond, Va., a four-year-old CDC — The Task Force for Historic Preservation

A renovated apartment in Jackson Ward, Richmond, Va. Many CDCs rebuild dilapidated housing for low-income residents, and also advise homeowners on property maintenance and keeping up mortgage payments.

and the Minority Community — is targeting its efforts on Jackson Ward, one of the most historic black neighborhoods in America. For inspiration and advice, the Task Force has looked to Savannah, Ga., where dramatic results are being achieved by the Savannah Landmark Rehabilitation Project, a nonprofit alliance of twenty-three white and black leaders founded by Leopold Adler II, an investment banker. Savannah Landmark in the mid-1970s adopted a breathtaking goal: to purchase and restore for low-income black tenants 600 of the 1,200 apartments and houses in the "Victorian District" — a forty-five-block area of wood-frame gingerbread houses fallen victim to slum landlords and disrepair. A decade later, hundreds of homes had been rehabilitated for poor Savannahans, cheek-by-jowl with the anticipated middle-class gentrification. From the houses' exteriors, it is virtually impossible to know the occupants' income status.

CDCs are not just an urban phenomenon. Some of the largest and oldest CDCs operate in rural areas, many covering a wide territory. The nineteen-year-old Community Enterprise Development Corporation of Alaska, for example, promotes rural development throughout the entire breadth of the country's largest state. Mississippi Action for Community Education targets its wide array of programs on forty counties in the Mississippi-Arkansas Delta region. The Mountain Association for Community Economic Development (MACED), with headquarters in Berea, Ky., has a target area spanning Central Appalachia. The Northern Community Investment Corporation in St. Johnsbury, Vt., focuses its development activities on the 185,000 residents of six impoverished rural counties in Vermont's "Northeast Kingdom" and New Hampshire's "North Country."

CDCs SIZE AND SCOPE

If one looks for a U.S.-wide focus on where CDCs are most likely to be found, the answers (with many exceptions) are: Especially prevalent in older cities of the Northeast and the Midwest. A few in major western cities. In a rural context, east of the Mississippi. The CDC movement has with a few very notable exceptions made less headway in the Great Plains, the Pacific Northwest, or in most southern cities.

Nationally, Boston and Chicago boast the most well-developed CDC networks, not just because each has a large number of CDCs, but also because of the advanced partnerships CDCs in these two cities have forged with local government and the business community. There are perhaps 100 community-based development groups in Chicago, a city with a tradition of neighborhood organizing, tough advocacy, and success at drawing city hall and private corporations into neighborhood issues. (Some of the heavy flow of capital into Chicago CDCs in the 1980s is the result of threatened legal action against banks under the 1977 Community Reinvestment Act.)

The strength of the CDC movement in Boston, on the other hand, is in no small part a reflection of the strong state support for CDCs initiated by Governor Michael Dukakis in the late 1970s. Since 1981 the number of Massachusetts CDCs has mushroomed from twelve to around seventy, about half of them in Boston.

Other cities with an advanced or growing CDC presence include New York, Philadelphia, Pittsburgh, Cleveland, Denver, Washington, D.C., Hartford, Miami, Indianapolis, St. Louis, Los Angeles, Minneapolis, Baltimore, Newark, Kansas City, San Francisco, Oakland, Cincinnati, Seattle, and Providence.

The more one examines CDCs, the more their infinite variety comes into focus. Although all try to assist less affluent Americans, the immediate target populations they serve vary broadly — Americans of every racial and ethnic stripe, women, farmers, American Indians, welfare recipients, small-business owners, juveniles, the homeless.

Moreover, the size and scope of CDCs vary as much as those of conventional businesses. Chicanos Por La Causa, organized in 1969 by a group of young Hispanic leaders in South Phoenix, now provides statewide service and has a staff of more than 100. Boston's Inquilinos Boricuas en Accion (Puerto Rican Tenants in Action) owns more than $50 million worth of real estate holdings in the city's South End, housing some 2,500 low-income Bostonians. The Community Enterprise Development Corporation of Alaska, through its wholly owned management company and subsidiaries, has annual gross sales of over $60 million.

But these are the exceptions. Most CDCs have only a few paid employees and operate on relative shoestrings. They rent space in modest offices; they rely on donated services from accountants, lawyers, and corporations; their yearly budgets probably average no higher than $200,000. Lucky is the CDC with more assets than a couple of typewriters, a computer, a copier, a coffee machine. And lots of folding chairs.

This run-down block in North Philadelphia typifies the kind of depressed area that CDCs are determined to bring back to life.

CHAPTER TWO

The First Generations

THE FIRST GENERATION CDCs: PIONEERING, EXPANSIVE

The 1960s: As middle-class America rushes to the suburbs, whole neighborhoods of northern cities, packed with southern black immigrants and their children, are becoming cauldrons of social discord.

The Bedford-Stuyvesant Restoration Corporation symbolizes the first, grand era of community development corporations. Into Brooklyn's five-mile-square Bed-Stuy section — with 450,000 people the nation's second largest black community — plagued by housing decay, school dropout, junkies, and muggers, comes a flood of investment dollars. Not for the typical poverty-program social services, but for hard investment, a new "business" approach to community development. The federal government and the Ford Foundation pour millions into the Bed-Stuy CDC. Banks and corporations pitch in; IBM opens a major plant in the neighborhood.

Visit Bed-Stuy twenty years later and there's pride, not depression, the sights and sounds of an energetic place. There's Restoration Plaza Commercial Center, a visible, central core the community never had before. Within the center are stores and offices, restaurants, two commercial banks, a supermarket, an ice skating rink, the Billie Holiday Theatre. The CDC has produced or renovated more than 1,600 units of housing, restored the exteriors of 4,200 homes on 150 blocks, provided mortgage assistance to 1,700 homeowners and loans and technical assistance to 130 local businesses. Some 16,000 jobs have been created. Some summers the CDC has hired as many as 1,500 young men and women — up on ladders and scaffolds, decked out in hard hats and tee-shirts, refurbishing as many as ten blocks of brownstones in a season.

True, social pathologies have not disappeared: now they crop up in such new forms as teenage pregnancies and the drug "crack." Unemployment is still a grave problem. Graffiti stains even some of the CDC's proud new structures. But Bed-Stuy has more: a new middle class. Young professionals have purchased brownstones, deciding to remain or return, becoming vital role models for their community. From restoring housing, then building a commercial core, Restoration has proceeded to the restoration of lives and the re-creation of a viable community.

The modern CDC movement was launched on the February day in 1966 when Senator Robert F. Kennedy toured the dilapidated streets of Bed-Stuy and planted the seeds for what would become the Bedford-Stuyvesant Restoration Corporation and the beginnings of federal involvement in CDCs. Kennedy was despondent over urban riots, just begun with Watts in 1965. His meetings with black leaders led him to an uneasy conclusion: there were fatal flaws, not just in the urban renewal of the 1950s but in all the liberal efforts to aid black and other poor Americans that had been catalyzed by his brother's presidency and pushed further with the Johnson administration's "war on poverty." The blacks Kennedy talked with as he walked the streets of Bedford-Stuyvesant had a clear message: stop studying us, show us something concrete — a supermarket, a place to shop. The idea emerged: rather than federal aid alone, rather than simply opening the doors to political participation of the poor, it was time to create new economic bases in troubled communities.

In 1966 Kennedy and his fellow New York senator, Jacob Javits, successfully sponsored an amendment to the 1964 Economic Opportunity Act — the bedrock legislation of President Johnson's "war on poverty" — to create the "Special Impact Program" for CDCs. From this sprang direct federal support to several dozen local organizations, urban and rural, scattered geographically, whose charge it was to combine social and economic programs to raise incomes, create jobs, and generate enterprises in poor neighborhoods.

Anxious to help was the Ford Foundation, which had already developed a "Gray Areas" strategy — the idea that poor communities have immense resources within them and, given a chance, the desire and the will to tackle their own social problems.

But it would be false to conclude that CDCs were an "invention" of the federal government, or the Ford Foundation. Both provided funds vital to the lift-off of the movement. But in fact its roots can be traced to the earliest American experiences — from the Mayflower Pilgrims with their compact of mutual assistance to the cooperatives of the Great Depression, from the Utopian communities of New Harmony and Oneida to Booker T. Washington and Marcus Garvey organizing collective business efforts to help former slaves after the Civil War. Writes Stewart Perry, a chronicler of the CDC movement:

> The conception was that being poor is not an individual affair but rather a systematic disease that afflicts whole communities. Deteriorated housing, impaired health, nonexistent or low wages, the welfare assault on self-respect, high crime rates, low tax base and reduced police and school services, child neglect and wife abuse, and always the continuing export of human and financial capital — all these feed on each other, . . . nest together to create the

impoverished community. [Thus the need for] a community-based and comprehensive approach to improving the local economy rather than trying desperately somehow to rebuild each individual so she or he can leave the impoverishing conditions behind....

By embracing community control and economic development, the early CDCs went beyond the federal, social-service orientation of the 1960s "war on poverty." But true to the spirit of their times, the first CDCs carried the aura of a grand social experiment. Many were sizable organizations, with expansive agendas and sometimes great expectations, dozens of full-time professionals and technical consultants, multi-year commitments for operational funds, massive housing projects, commercial ventures, social service programs, venture capital arms, even trusts.

The roots of some of the early CDCs lay in the bulldog advocacy tactics of the famed Chicago-based community organizer Saul Alinsky. A prime example was The Woodlawn Organization (TWO), formed in 1959 as a federation of some 100 community groups on the South Side of Chicago, fighting landlord-tenant battles and trying to press more social services out of Mayor Richard Daley's entrenched political machine. TWO tried to befriend and domesticate such street gangs as the Blackstone Rangers and the Devil's Disciples and as its reward got a hostile probe by Arkansas Senator John McClellan's Senate Investigations Committee. But by the late 1960s TWO had opened its own supermarket and was rehabilitating hundreds of dilapidated Chicago brownstones and building a 502-unit apartment complex. TWO's housing proved infinitely superior, in its sense of order, cleanliness, and tenant security, to the gargantuan, chaotic public housing projects run by the Chicago Housing Authority.

Another CDC root was religious. In the early 1960s, Philadelphia's Rev. Leon Sullivan started a youth-employment service in his Zion Baptist Church but became enraged by the city's continuing wall of segregation, which kept blacks out of any but the most menial jobs. Sullivan organized black ministers to launch boycotts against firms that spurned black applicants. As the campaign succeeded and jobs opened, he organized the Opportunities Industrialization Center (later to spread to more than 100 cities, even abroad) to train black youth for the world of work. He persuaded his parishioners to contribute $10 a month to create a capital base for community education, local housing, and economic development. In time, the federal government, the Ford Foundation, and Philadelphia banks and insurance firms were contributing millions to Sullivan projects ranging from a major shopping center to new housing and an electronics plant. By the early 1970s Sullivan's CDC was supporting over 4,000 people in its vast network and spending a budget in excess of $50 million annually. Sullivan became the first black member of the General Motors board of directors.

In Pittsburgh's East Liberty neighborhood, CDC workers dig up a pedestrian mall, an urban renewal experiment from the 1960s that failed to attract shoppers or businesses. Restoring commercial strips is a major activity of many CDCs.

In Los Angeles, the spread-out, palm-lined streets of Watts witnessed in 1965 the first of the decade's great riots: a sickening four-day orgy of destruction and death, injuring over 1,000 people, taking thirty-four lives, causing over $40 million in damage. In its wake, a new CDC, the Watts Labor Community Action Committee, got started with critical support from the United Auto Workers. WLCAC was soon running job-training programs for youth, building big quantities of housing, operating supermarkets, gas stations, a restaurant, and "dial-a-ride" transit services for senior citizens. Its leader was erstwhile auto worker Ted Watkins, a husky, barrel-chested ex-Mississippi farm kid who would still be leading WLCAC two decades later.

Bed-Stuy, TWO, Zion, WLCAC, and their sister CDCs — the Spanish-Speaking Unity Council, the Kentucky Highlands Investment Corporation, Mississippi Action for Community Education, among them — received major funds from the federal government through the Office of Economic Opportunity or the Model Cities program. Philanthropic support, Ford in the lead, was substantial, and the savviest CDCs emulated Sullivan's success in drawing big corporate dollars.

However impressive the birth of the first CDCs in the 1960s, there were fewer than 100 in all by New Year's Day 1970. Some of the early experiments eventually fell on hard times; a few folded. TWO lost its supermarket; electronics manufacture in North Philadelphia faltered. A handful of CDCs were plagued by mismanagement, even scandal. For example, the *Los Angeles Times* printed stories asserting that the leaders of The East Los Angeles Community Union (TELACU) were living too well and misusing federal funds. Though defenders said the charges were ill-founded — and TELACU did go on to manage many substantive and worthwhile projects — the incident raised a red flag for community development activists.

Actual abuse in CDCs was, however, a rarity. Considering how hostile ghettos and barrios and poor rural places were thought to be to any form of economic development, the CDC movement advanced at a healthy clip, in some cases with remarkable rapidity. In less than half a decade, the new model of economic base building for society's least fortunate had gained a firm foothold. As the nation tired of its "war on poverty," the community-led forces for economic development were just getting started.

A trolley barn in the East Liberty section of Pittsburgh that will be converted to shops.

THE SECOND GENERATION: LEANER, WIDELY DIVERSE

The 1970s: Freeways come plowing through urban neighborhoods, pushed by a suburbanized middle class, center-city business interests, and the highway lobby. A ferociously determined neighborhood movement forms.

In Boston, residents of overwhelmingly black Jamaica Plain mobilize to stop I-95, a connecting link from central Boston to the Route 128 beltway. They win; neighborhood opposition has killed a major U.S. expressway.

But how to assure commercial development and a sure supply of jobs for residents along the corridor of the new rapid transit line being constructed through Jamaica Plain? How to restore faith in the real estate market after the blow of eminent domain and demolition? How to get additional housing, recreation and park facilities?

Planning begins: Several hundred community residents meet to pinpoint problems, set priorities, and organize their own CDC. In 1977 the Neighborhood Development Corporation of Jamaica Plain starts operations. Money comes from the state of Massachusetts, the National Trust for Historic Preservation, the Local Initiatives Support Corporation, Boston banks, the federal Economic Development Administration, and the federal Office of Community Services. A historic brick brewery complex of sixteen buildings on five acres, former home of Pickwick Ale and Haffenreffer Malt, is rehabilitated, piece by piece, for small businesses and one big tenant (Boston Beer, producer of Sam Adams Beer). The old Jamaica Plain High School is converted to Sumner Hill House, seventy-five units of mixed-income housing. A vacant nursing home is transformed into family-style living for the elderly. From tough neighborhood advocacy, defending the home turf, the focus turns to grass-roots economic development: a story repeated coast to coast.

Hundreds of new CDCs sprang up in the 1970s, as a remarkably diverse range of community organizations began to apply the CDC approach on a more modest scale than the first generation. Like Jamaica Plain, many had their roots in neighborhood self-consciousness. The struggles were not just against freeways, but against blockbusting and redlining, indiscriminate city-ordered demolitions, inadequate city services, and university land-grabs in vulnerable urban neighborhoods.

Some among the CDC second wave grew out of nonprofit organizations that had formed to take advantage of federal supports for low-income housing. Others evolved out of social service organizations and the community action agencies that the federal Office of Economic Opportunity (OEO), beginning in the 1960s, had inspired by the hundreds. Indian tribes, a few banks, even a corporation or two moved to form CDCs. And then there were numerous CDCs organized to serve the influx of new Hispanic and Asian immigrants.

East Bay Asian Local Development Corp. in Oakland, Calif., typifies the second generation CDC. It was formed in 1975 to serve the city's growing population of Chinese, Japanese, Filipinos, Koreans, Vietnamese, Cambodians, and Laotians. As its first project, East Bay Asian transformed a deteriorated warehouse in Oakland's Chinatown into a thriving Asian Resource Center. The market-rate rents charged commercial tenants — among them a pharmacy, an accounting firm, and a Bank of America branch — finance a comprehensive array of social services, ranging from vocational training and job placement to immigration counseling and refugee business assistance. East Bay Asian is no stranger to failure. Its first business enterprise, Vericlean Janitorial Service, had to be closed in 1986. But the CDC has gone on to create its own revolving loan fund for area entrepreneurs, and to undertake the construction of 119 new units of rental housing and the rehabilitation of an abandoned hotel.

Like their predecessors of the 1960s, the CDCs born in the 1970s could count on the help of a broad array of federal programs. CDCs continued to receive millions of dollars annually from their own special federal agency, the Community Services Administration, created in 1974 as OEO's successor. By 1978 another important CDC supporter, HUD's Office of Neighborhood Development, had arrived on the scene.

But support for CDCs did not stop there. Explains Andrew Mott of the Center for Community Change: "Although the Carter Administration never developed a coherent policy of support for grass-roots organizations, by 1980 there were over a dozen federal programs providing important sources of support for local staff and projects." Furthermore, he adds, "an increasing number of foundations and corporations were making serious commitments to community groups."

Thus, in housing, education and training, health, criminal justice, economic development, even agriculture, community-based development groups were aggressively being sought out as effective delivery agents. By 1980 more than 1,000 CDCs had exploded on the scene in every corner of the nation. Technical sophistication in the leveraging of public and private resources was on the rise. New and different types of projects, some remarkably innovative, were receiving assistance. A few states, Massachusetts in the lead, had begun developing their own programs to promote CDCs. And in communities across the country, from Boston and Hartford to Cleveland, Chicago, and San Francisco, a brawny new neighborhood movement, grown dramatically over the 1970s, found its fate integrally linked with CDCs. Community economic development was no longer a tentative, alternative way to help poor communities; it was fast becoming *the* chosen vehicle.

A revitalized commercial strip in Pittsburgh's Homewood-Brushton section. The local CDC *provides loans to small businesses and trains their owners in business management.*

CHAPTER THREE

CDCs in the 1980s:
Reassessing the "Marketplace"

The 1980s: the decade of the Reagan Presidency. The federal government cuts back sharply on assistance to depressed urban and rural America. The federal Community Services Administration, major funder of CDCs, is dismantled. So is HUD's short-lived Office of Neighborhood Development. The Comprehensive Employment and Training Act, which through its contracts and publicly funded job slots had supported many CDC staffs and organizers, gives way to a scaled-down Jobs Training Partnership Act, to support training only. Subsidies for low-income housing production are decimated. Urban Development Action Grants are shrunken; so are budgets for the Economic Development Administration and numerous antipoverty programs. CDCs scurry to form new partnerships with private business, local government, and local and national foundations.

Once a middle-to-upper-class white neighborhood with a flourishing commercial center, Pittsburgh's Homewood-Brushton section has come on hard times. Many stores are boarded up; capital has fled. Graffiti and abandonment are painfully evident. Of the 16,000 people, 97 percent are black, mostly poor.

In 1982 community and business groups form the Homewood-Brushton Revitalization and Development Corporation and hire to run it Mulugetta Birru, a former high-ranking Ethiopian government official and graduate of Syracuse University's Maxwell School of Citizenship.

A short history, a long list of accomplishments. By 1987 this CDC has initiated development of its first apartments and thirty-three town houses. It has a revolving loan fund for small businesses spurned by local banks. Its sewing cooperative provides jobs for thirty women who turn out wedding and prom gowns. A franchise deal for a Dairy Queen is in the works, a mini-mall on the drawing boards. The CDC trains local entrepreneurs in business management; it has a neighborhood watch and a business-safety program; it sponsors festivals and consumer fairs and a monthly newspaper.

And the funding? Major operating funds come from a consortium made up of the Ford Foundation, which had started a major new program for emerging CDCs, the city of Pittsburgh, the Howard Heinz Endowment, and the Mellon Bank Foundation. Special housing assistance is provided by the Enterprise Foundation and the Commonwealth of Pennsylvania. Monies also flow from a special city fund of repaid UDAG (Urban Development Action Grant) loans. Conspicuously absent: major federal subsidy.

Homewood-Brushton's CDC is not an exception, an anomaly in the era of Reaganomics and severely restricted federal budgets. In point of fact, more than 1,000 new CDCs have emerged since 1981. Organizationally, the movement more than doubled in five years.

"I find these organizations enormously productive," says Joseph McNeely, president of the Development Training Institute, the country's premier trainer of CDC leaders. "They are accomplishing projects requiring greater skill and complexity than anybody thought possible in the 1970s, and without all the kinds of resources they should have and need."

"CDCs have reassessed the marketplace," says Brenda Shockley, director of the Drew Economic Development Corp. in Los Angeles. "Now we are understanding what will fly in this climate — and what won't."

"Today you have to find ways to resemble the real for-profit world," adds Joe Giron, director of Brothers Redevelopment Inc. in Denver. "Otherwise, you won't be around."

Guillermo Salas, director of the Hispanic Association of Contractors and Entrepreneurs, a Philadelphia CDC, sums up the new style this way: "We no longer take a 'gimme, gimme' attitude. Now we are learning how to infiltrate into the system. We've learned to be much more creative."

And from Federico Pena, the mayor of Denver, seedbed of significant CDC growth in the 1980s, comes this assessment: "Generally speaking, the CDCs we have worked with are competent, professional, have done their homework, and understand the process very well. They can make presentations you'd normally hear only from a corporate CEO."

So it is that CDCs, young and old alike, are exhibiting business talent and development skills once thought to be the exclusive province of the for-profit sector. They are learning how to pursue targeted objectives and make tough, well-grounded choices about priorities. "Being nonprofit doesn't mean you don't make money," quips Brenda Shockley. "It means no individual gets to keep the money."

Many in the movement view CDCs' new bottom-line approach as an advantage over earlier CDC efforts, which sometimes collapsed when their sponsors unwittingly loaded these fledgling organizations with too many, sometimes competing, goals — creating jobs, making profits, managing business ventures, delivering services, providing training, empowering the community, and many others.

Others note, too, how remarkably entrepreneurial CDCs of the 1980s have become in forging partnerships with local governments and the widening number of corporations willing to answer the call for more "socially responsive" investment. This, they say, has the advantage of broadening CDCs' base of support, breaking over-reliance on federal funding.

Many of today's CDCs are becoming adept at hooking into the 1980s' culture of small business, entrepreneurial growth, and building a capacity for indigenous economic development in communities long plagued by poverty and dependency. For proof, one need only examine the changes in prevailing CDC strategies for generating jobs. During the 1960s and 1970s, CDCs focused largely on trying to start their own businesses. Many failed. Few ever became very profitable or produced the hoped-for level of jobs. Today's CDCs, by contrast, are more likely to supply equity capital, loans, incubator space, and technical assistance in support of home-grown private entrepreneurs and businesses in their midst. Even when they do start their own enterprises, CDCs are more carefully looking to enter potentially profitable "market" niches, turning to growth industries such as cable television, day care, and senior citizen services, or establishing franchises of national restaurant, rent-a-car, automotive services, and other chains.

A paradigm of the times is the Northern Community Investment Corporation (NCIC) in St. Johnsbury, Vt. It began life in 1975 with a development strategy firmly rooted in starting its own businesses. But before long, poor results and heavy dependency on shrinking federal resources necessitated a shift in strategy. So NCIC became a venture capitalist and loan provider. By 1987 the CDC had invested in more than 165 businesses, with a combined annual payroll of over $22 million. The investments ranged from a $10,000 loan to help an entrepreneur buy an ailing farm machinery firm to $950,000 in equity to reopen a Lisbon, N.H. shoe factory that today employs 241 workers. All told, NCIC is credited with having created or saved 1,931 area jobs; its investment portfolio is worth some $8 million. More important, NCIC has leveraged an additional $54 million in financing for its firms, mostly from private institutions, a significant portion of that from outside the CDC target area. NCIC carefully monitors the management capacity of the firms it invests in, enlisting when needed experts from the federal Small Business Administration or universities to provide technical assistance. NCIC's activities aren't limited just to businesses: it has also developed more than $13.5 million worth of real estate.

Although many note that CDCs' growing business acumen holds tremendous promise for widening CDC impact, other crosscurrents in the marketplace of the 1980s may not bode so well. One especially thorny problem is the scarcity of dollars for CDC core operating expenses. The major share of the increased funding from the private sector and other new CDC partners has been for "projects." Federal project dollars, albeit shrunken, still flow. But the large, multi-year grants that catalyzed earlier generations of CDCs — enabling them to hire staff, develop agendas, educate the community about CDC activities, and otherwise support basic CDC operations — are as scarce as country clubs in the ghetto. Foundations and a handful of state and local governments have picked up some of the slack. But the universe of competing CDCs has grown so large that it has outstripped the capacity of its existing supporters to provide sufficient funds for operating expenses.

Says Thomas Miller, head of the Ford Foundation's Program-Related Investment office and former director of the Kentucky Highlands CDC: "In the early days, CDCs had lots of money and little capacity. Now there's lots of capacity and too little money."

For many of the older CDCs, accommodation has been difficult. A few have been forced to shut down; many have curtailed programs. The flagship Bed-Stuy CDC is still recovering from its loss of $4 million a year in federal administrative support. The eighteen-year-old Community Development Corporation of Kansas City at one time received some $450,000 annually from the Community Services Administration, using the grant to hire a twenty-two-member staff of specialists and consultants in marketing, real estate, financial analysis, and business management. The funding stopped just as the organization was preparing to expand its highly successful minority business-development program. The CDC has adjusted, says executive director Donald Maxwell, by restructuring, paring its staff to five, using more consultants, brokering services, and learning to leverage scarce dollars for wider impact.

For the CDCs emerging in the 1980s, the dearth of funding for operating expenses has obliged many to become so project-oriented that some longtime CDC supporters fear they may be giving short shrift to such traditional CDC goals as developing minority leaders or empowering poor residents. The more technocratic orientation, some say, threatens to weaken CDC constituency support. "Some CDCs may end up becoming development corporations in search of a neighborhood," says Graham Finney, a consultant who evaluates CDC performance.

Others worry, too, that in the rush to do projects, today's CDCs may be ignoring other important aspects of economic development. "Projects probably constitute no more than 10 percent of community development," says Pablo Eisenberg, president of the Washington, D.C.-based Center for Community Change. He's concerned that too many CDCs shy away from confrontation on such major issues as how massive public subsidies are used, how credit is allocated, and who makes crucial zoning and infrastructure decisions. Cumulatively, he says, these issues may have far more impact on a community than individual economic development projects.

Some also note that the third-generation CDCs appear less "activist" than their predecessors. Just to exist, they have to engage in virtually nonstop fund raising. Then they face the administrative nightmare of conceiving and carrying out complex development projects with multiple partners. Each negotiation may present major obstacles; foot-dragging by any one partner

A North Philadelphia garbage recycling plant organized by the local CDC. Here, as in other communities, CDCs help create jobs for local residents.

can imperil a larger project. Another factor: closer association with the private sector and local government may discourage advocacy. Few organizations are anxious to alienate new-found funding partners.

Some CDCs have made an artful transition. Philadelphia's West Oak Lane is a lower-middle-class neighborhood that suffered blockbusting and massive housing abandonment as its population switched from Jewish to black. First on the scene, in the late 1970s, was an Alinsky-style protest group, fighting redlining by the banks. In time that group split into warring camps and, in the words of one local observer, "self-exploded." But not without progeny: the West Oak Lane Community Development Corporation, founded in 1980, began to rehabilitate the neighborhood's 600 abandoned houses. From the outset the CDC acted as a general contractor with its own construction crew, rehabbing chiefly single-family homes under contract with the city. In 1983 it expanded into rental units, acquiring ownership of some $1 million worth of properties in the neighborhood. By the mid-1980s it had broadened its focus to business development, opening its own Dunkin Donuts franchise, which has created some twenty-five new jobs and, the CDC hopes, will supply a steady stream of income to help fund its other activities.

"In the 1970s we were activists, mostly out of the civil rights movement," notes West Oak Lane director Jan Rubin, describing the changes she has observed in CDCs. Some of that continues: the West Oak Lane CDC has taken to task Philadelphia's city government on such issues as placing lucrative overnight deposits with banks that lack branches in the neighborhoods.

But in general, says Rubin, CDCs of the 1980s are less confrontational. "We may be tending now, with more Harvard and Wharton grads, to be approaching development with less 'political' sense. It may be creating a complacency among us," she continues. "It's harder to fight with a Sun Oil or a Bell Tel when you want to look and act like them."

Tough advocacy has hardly disappeared, however. Gale Cincotta, founder of National People's Action, the neighborhood-based lobby whose anti-redlining crusade led to the Community Reinvestment Act of 1977, in 1984 joined with allies in the new Chicago Reinvestment Alliance (CRA) to force merger-prone Chicago banks to earmark $173 million for low-income housing investment. The funds have proven an immense boon to Chicago's CDCs, and the same CRA challenge tactic is being applied in other cities. Elsewhere, CDCs that might fear reprisals if they single-handedly took on governments or major financial institutions appear less reluctant to do so in groups. In Denver, for instance, a coalition of CDCs and nonprofits, "Fifty for Housing," successfully pressed the city government to devote to low-income housing half of its $22 million dollar "Skyline" fund, capitalized with the interest payments from a huge downtown redevelopment fund.

Community leaders do still differ, sometimes sharply, on what they believe is the best focus — advocacy or specific development projects. But there are indications that the gap between the two schools may be narrowing. William Duncan, president of the Mountain Association for Community Economic Development in Kentucky, says the dichotomy is "obsolete," a "red herring." It's not sufficient, he says, "to be happy in the sandbox and have projects that work and people pat you on the back." Conversely, he goes on, organizing can be self-defeating if it comes across as "shrill or politically and fiscally irrational."

Duncan maintains: "You have to conceive of fundamental mainstream change of how the economy works as your goal." In his view, too few CDCs do that. They must, he says, extend efforts well beyond individual projects to, when necessary, moving state governments, city councils, corporations, and banking establishments to comprehensive investment approaches in communities long left out of the action.

CDCs can increase their net power, Duncan believes, when they "put advocacy and development traditions together. We can become development technicians with a political orientation and political activists with technical development skills."

The manager of an employee-owned and -operated supermarket built with the help of a CDC in North Philadelphia. CDCs foster a range of business skills among community residents.

CHAPTER FOUR

Scale: The Critical Challenge

March 1985: It is a dazzling Saturday morning in Miami's Liberty City. Families dressed in their Sunday best stand in line for an experience commonplace for most Americans — shopping at a well-stocked supermarket.

Inside the sparkling new Winn-Dixie store in Edison Plaza, beaming, courteous teenagers — the boys in white shirts and black ties, girls in blue uniforms — run cash registers, stock shelves, and help customers with their first chance in five years to buy quality groceries in their neighborhood.

The nation's last glimpse of this block, in 1981, had been quite different: a National Guardsman in riot gear, armed with an automatic rifle, holding four black teenagers at bay. In that scene, the old grocery store was a gutted shell. Produce bins, beer cans, and broken bottles floated in a sea of water left by firefighters. Food displays hung eerily from the ceiling, advertising yesterday's specials. The site — like most of Liberty City — seemed jinxed, suggested another riot waiting to happen.

What powerful force transformed Liberty City? It was a CDC — the Tacolcy Economic Development Corporation, in league with an impressive array of funding partners: the Ford Foundation and the city of Miami; the Local Initiatives Support Corporation and the federal Economic Development Administration; city business leaders and Winn-Dixie itself, which invested $2 million.

Today, the white stucco and red brick Edison Plaza has added a dry-cleaning shop, pharmacy, beauty parlor, and shoe store. In offices behind the store, a law firm and a security company have moved in. McDonald's has opened across the way. The New Beginning shopping center nearby has ten small shops, and two blocks away the CDC has broken ground for a $5.2 million apartment complex with 121 units.

And the residents? "There is a real sense of pride in what has happened here," says Otis Pitts, the ex-cop who is Tacolcy's executive director. "It's not like people just coming to shop in a store. It's like they're coming to something that is a vital part of their community."

Says a local merchant, owner of People's Barber Shop: "We don't only look good, we are good. Now everybody is committed to staying in this neighborhood. Why leave now? We sweated out the worst. Ain't nothing to do but look forward now."

Scale, scale, scale. That is what the Tacolcy Economic Development Corporation and its partners are seeking to realize with Edison Plaza. By working to reverse Liberty City's highly negative image, they are paving the way for development in an area where standard government-sponsored revival tactics and a disjointed set of loans to black businesses had come to naught.

The question of scale, of critical impact, has returned to the front burner of CDC concerns in the 1980s. In a sense, it represents a return to the first years of the CDC movement when the Ford- and federally backed CDCs had no less an ambition. Some in fact succeeded — Bedford-Stuyvesant and Mississippi Action for Community Education, among others — in effecting highly significant changes in their target areas. They brought about change considerably beyond "marginal" — the term critics are prone to throw at the CDC movement.

The movement's leaders believe the challenge of the coming years is to build on the thousands of small CDC "miracles" of the 1960s, 1970s, and 1980s toward broad, long-term community impact. As one example of the direction of the times, Ford Foundation president Franklin A. Thomas points to the intensified effort of the 1980s to make such mainline community institutions as schools, hospitals, and banks full partners in CDC development. "Now," says Thomas, "we have a sufficiently broad experience to go for scale."

Though they frequently intersect, there are three principal schools of thought on how CDCs can move to greater scale in American life:

> by large, symbolic projects that begin to reverse a community's negative image;
> by the numbers: catalyzing CDC activity to a point where the efforts in housing rehabilitation or job creation reach a cumulatively massive scale;
> by strategic political and economic interventions.

LARGE, SYMBOLIC PROJECTS

Liberty City's Edison Plaza is a prime example of a dramatic project that telegraphs the message: "This community is turning around." So is the Linwood Shopping Center, opened in 1986 in a tough part of Kansas City. The center was developed by the Community Development Corporation of Kansas City, in partnership with the city's influential Black Ministers Union, on the site of a huge abandoned hospital. (Just having that massive structure demolished proved to be a media event. Film crews for the ABC-TV movie *The Day After* used the explosion to portray the aftershocks of a nuclear holocaust.) The ministers undertook the task of mobilizing community backing while the CDC took responsibility for planning and overseeing the project, searching out commercial tenants, arranging the financing.

Feasibility studies revealed that what the neighborhood needed most was a quality supermarket, that some $76 million annually was flowing out of the community and into the cash registers of suburban groceries. Associated Grocers, a major chain, agreed to be the center's anchor store; other commitments followed — from Revco Drugs, Goodyear Tires, Payless Shoes, Hallmark Cards, Burger King, Popeyes. Complex financing was painstakingly assembled — from the federal government, the city, private investors, Prudential Insurance Co., Centerre Bank, Boatman's Bank, the Local Initiatives Support Corporation, and the Hallmark, Ford, and Capital Cities foundations. The public-private cooperation behind the effort helped Kansas City win an "All America Cities" award in 1985.

And the center *has* had direct economic impact: some 275 new jobs, mostly entry level, nearly all filled by residents of the CDC's target area. By 10:30 a.m. any day, the center is teeming with shoppers; by afternoon, the 375-car parking lot is filled to capacity. Early in 1987, the CDC began acquiring land and forging pre-leasing agreements for a second major center, Linwood Square, across the street.

BY THE NUMBERS

Concentrating on shelter for low-income people, CDCs in some cities find the sheer number of units they have brought on line reaching a level of significant scale. In Boston, officials report that some 80 percent of the city's new low-cost housing in the past two years is CDC built. Some of that is the result of an innovative consortium, the Boston Housing Partnership, initiated in 1983. Within three years it had rehabilitated 700 units of low-income housing and was well along on plans to produce 1,000 more. The method: combining the special housing skills and community ties of CDCs operating in ten separate neighborhoods with the skills and resources of local banks, businesses, and the city government. As the units come on line, the CDCs handle the difficult tasks of tenant selection, rent collection, and maintenance — tasks the government and private-sector partners determined could be far better performed by neighborhood-based organizations than public agencies.

CDCs have become prolific housing producers in other cities as well — in Chicago, New York, and Cleveland, where partnerships similar to Boston's have started, and in Denver, St. Louis, and Minneapolis. With the federal government's construction subsidies virtually terminated, nonprofits have become the low-income housing industry in the United States. "One thing we can say with assuredness," notes Barry Zigas of the Low Income Housing Information Service. "*All* the innovative housing work today is at the nonprofit level."

In whatever quantities they can manage, all but a tiny portion of CDCs are doing at least some housing; for many, it is the primary focus. The reasons are obvious enough. Housing ranks high on the list of needs in any poor area. Ailing neighborhoods remain fertile ground in which to secure housing stock or abandoned property at very low or undervalued cost, often from the city's tax-delinquent rolls or federal government foreclosures. Real estate offers excellent opportunities for building a CDC's wealth and collateral, for honing development skills, and for establishing a track record with which to approach banks, corporations, and other would-be funders. A not insignificant factor is the growing financial — and political — support many local governments lend to CDC-sponsored real estate reclamation.

Nor do bricks and mortar tell the whole story. Most CDCs are complementing their "hard" real estate development activities with programs to help low-income renters buy their own homes. Many assist homeowners in maintaining their properties, keeping up payments, and avoiding foreclosures.

Along with their push for scale, some CDCs are finding creative ways to link real estate development with social services, training, or employment programs. New CDC housing complexes have begun to include day-care centers so that parents of small children can work. In Denver, Brothers Redevelopment Director Joe Giron worked out a deal to allow public high school "shop" students, as part of their curriculum, to join Brothers' work crews rehabilitating dilapidated housing stock. Next, Giron persuaded Denver judges to send youthful first-time offenders to work on his construction crews instead of to jail — a strategy that annually nets 25,000 hours of free labor on the CDC projects.

Can CDCs achieve scale by the sheer numbers in job creation as well as in housing? The record indicates far less success. But there are glowing exceptions, especially among the rural CDCs. One is in the Mississippi Delta region, where a plantation economy survived a full century after Reconstruction, leaving black field hands and their families desperately poor and ill-educated. Growing out of Mississippi's dramatic civil rights struggles of the 1960s, the Delta Foundation and its sister organization, Mississippi Action for Community Education, have since 1969 created more than 1,000 jobs and generated over $30 million in new income in the Delta. Led until his death in 1986 by Charles Bannerman, a particularly aggressive black leader, Delta spun off one subsidiary after another (at one time it had forty-six!). Manufacturing ranged from blue jeans to railway spikes to pull-down attic stairs to rice cakes, some of the enterprises closing, others opening, with shifts in national market demand. The CDC's venture capital arm has funded dozens of independent small businesses and helped black lawyers and doctors start their practices. In 1986 the organization also launched a small-business incubator for women entrepreneurs.

*A welder for a Denver CDC finishing a
window gate that will be installed in housing for the elderly.*

In eastern Kentucky, a chronically depressed area of Appalachia, the Kentucky Highlands Investment Corporation, founded in 1970, has supplied capital, loans, and business advice to small, low-technology and labor-intensive manufacturers of such products as kayaks, sleeping bags, coal-truck beds, and stuffed animals. By 1986, 1,250 new jobs had been created, and some 200 were being added each year. The CDC was showing $1 million in annual profits. Though it had received heavy federal and foundation support over the years, Kentucky Highlands' net worth of nearly $12 million exceeded the total of all grants it had ever received.

Alaska has a statewide CDC — the Community Enterprise Development Corporation (CEDC) of Alaska — that claims to have created nearly 4,000 jobs since its founding in 1968. The jobs are in every field, from cooperative stores to reindeer processing, from housing weatherization to seafood marketing. CEDC's membership consists of more than 100 rural, community-based organizations representing chiefly Eskimos and Indians. CEDC has financed fishing and retail cooperatives in numerous small villages; it owns its own statewide merchandise chain. And CEDC offers intensive technical assistance and has its own for-profit subsidiary overseeing its equity investments.

It may be no accident that the CDCs achieving scale in job creation are active in depressed rural areas where the economic pulse beats faintest. Says Tom Miller, former director of Kentucky Highlands and now at Ford: "It takes a long time to get up to speed in economic development. It may take twenty years before you see results. But today there may be as many as ten self-sufficient organizations in backwater areas that are beginning to generate enough results to say they'll eventually make a real difference."

BY STRATEGIC INTERVENTION

A final CDC strategy for achieving scale involves critical political and economic interventions. The idea is to target limited resources to leverage broader investments from others; to press major economic institutions to alter some of their practices affecting low-income communities; and to use the political process where appropriate. Though distinctly different from the familiar CDC route of direct housing and job creation, strategic intervention is becoming increasingly popular within the movement.

"A CDC should never have small concepts of what it can accomplish," insists William Duncan, president of the Mountain Association for Community Economic Development in Kentucky. He cites MACED's own strategy of "sectoral intervention" as a prime example. In 1981 the CDC created a forest products center, hired a hardwoods industry expert to run it, and saturated itself with intricate knowledge of the industry. MACED's analysis revealed that lumber was a good source of entrepreneurial opportunity for farmers, laid-off miners, and small-scale loggers — excellent targets for CDC assistance. MACED first tried financing individual lumber mill projects. The strategy didn't work; mired in deal-by-deal intricacies, it proved extraordinarily time-consuming and produced few jobs. But the group's research suggested an alternative. Most of the small lumber mills faced persistent problems in selling their products, especially their high-grade, more profitable woods, in the highly volatile hardwoods marketplace. MACED's solution: create a CDC subsidiary — Ridgecrest Enterprises — to buy lumber from the small producers, stockpile it, then resell it on national markets.

MACED underwent a similar searching to determine how best to make available more affordable mortgages for Kentucky home buyers. "First we considered starting our own savings and loan," Duncan explains, "but it didn't take much insight to realize that would not have much impact. Next we considered forming a mortgage banking company, which would be more far-reaching and involve less overhead." Finally, the organization decided to go the advocacy route. "We formed a consortium of ninety-six banks to work to change their prevailing mortgage-lending practices. Now the dominant mortgage available to eastern Kentucky homebuyers is a thirty-year, 5 percent down, fixed-rate, low-interest loan." To change Kentucky banks' lending practices, Duncan said, took "our same budget, one staff person, and two years. It cost us far less money than doing fifteen units of housing under HUD's Section 8 and it will have a lot more effect."

No one has ever defined when benefits move from incremental to major, or what represents true "scale." But when an Edison Plaza remakes the image of Liberty City, or when block after block of a poor community gets new or rehabilitated housing, or when a rural CDC over the years provides thousands of jobs in areas of chronic unemployment, CDCs move from glowing small examples to the threshold of a critical contribution to American life.

Brenda Shockley, an attorney and director of the Drew Economic Development Corp. in Los Angeles. Drew has developed low- to moderate-income housing that incorporates child-care facilities.

CHAPTER FIVE

Architects of a New Society

Brenda Shockley. A power résumé. Occidental College, Howard and Loyola Law schools, stints in land development, the Los Angeles City Attorney's office, administrative assistant to top L.A. politician Yvonne Brathwaite Burke, for five years a partner in a private law firm. In 1981 the dean of the Drew Medical School — with the Martin Luther King Jr. Hospital one of two big medical facilities brought into Watts after the notorious 1965 riots — prevails on Shockley to be his point person on community outreach. Within a year she has formed a CDC with heavy Drew involvement. Funders from state to county governments, Ford to local foundations find her intellect, plans, hard to resist. Financing of $3.5 million is assembled for Willowbrook Green, a low-to-moderate-income housing development on Drew's land, targeted to single-parent families (medical residents, neighborhood people). But not ordinary housing: central to the plans is a sophisticated eighteen-hour-a-day child-care center employing Drew's expertise and child-development staff.

Gary Waldron. South Bronx native, holds a master's degree in industrial behavior, gets on the fast track at IBM, becomes a comptroller. On the side, Waldron is on the board of Group Live-In Experience (GLIE), which runs a home for runaway youths. In 1979 he takes a year's leave from IBM to help at GLIE full time; he returns to IBM in 1980 — for six days. "I knew I was good enough to run IBM, and knew they'd never let me. I had this crazy idea about agriculture on all that abandoned South Bronx land." The result: GLIE Farms, growing fancy herbs — from chervil to chives, tarragon to thyme — servicing New York's premier restaurants, via subway delivery, with hours-fresh produce. Waldron's salary is $20,000, compared to $60,000 at IBM. GLIE experiences ups and downs. To the rescue: the Port of Authority of New York and New Jersey, which stakes GLIE to a $1.2 million hydroponic greenhouse — Dutch design tried first time in the United States, herbs grown in water-soaked rock wool with computer-controlled nutrient flow. The business expands to 1,000 customers. GLIE obtains a farm in Puerto Rico to mass-produce herbs, using Israeli production techniques, flying the produce to New York for packaging and distribution. GLIE expands into edible flowers, miniature vegetables, reaches $8 million in sales, creates its own R and D unit, prepares to franchise herb greenhouses to CDCs across the country.

Ruby Duncan. Welfare mother turned entrepreneur. Divorced in 1965, Duncan gets a job as a pantry worker in Las Vegas's swanky Sahara Hotel to support her seven children. One day she steps in a puddle of grease, is seriously injured, has to stay home for a year, ends up on welfare. She joins the Clark County Welfare Rights Organization, and in 1971 helps lead a march of 4,000 welfare mothers down Las Vegas's main casino strip, demanding a reversal of deep state welfare cuts. A year later the women form Operation Life to promote health care and jobs in a west Las Vegas neighborhood blighted by boarded-up store fronts, shunned by supermarkets, shopping centers, and banks. By the late 1970s Operation Life is a CDC, subsidized by the federal Community Services Administration and several religious groups. It starts a medical center that by 1987 will be serving 75,000 patients a year. It builds housing units, buys an abandoned downtown hotel for rehabilitation, plans a seventy-acre industrial park. Have these new capitalists lost their earlier fervor? Apparently not. "We're still into advocacy," says Duncan. "There ain't going to be any downtown development unless we get our share of the action."

Charles Duff. Erstwhile Latin teacher, descendant of an old Baltimore family, graduate of Amherst College and Harvard University with training in city planning. Duff finds a planning job in a suburban Baltimore county rather boring, casts about for more challenging work, and ends up with southwest Baltimore's COIL — Communities Organized to Improve Life. Partly it's a way to fulfill his hobby, rehabbing houses. COIL, a kind of social service conglomerate, was formed by forty-three community associations. One part of COIL is into advocacy; another focuses on senior care, adult literacy classes, and programs for troubled youth. Duff's division, a CDC specializing in real estate development, can take credit for rehabbing sixty-five homes, providing financing for thirty home buyers, and brokering mortgages for some 200 others. Duff proceeds to develop a day-care center for seniors where working people can drop off their frail parents for the day, as well as new quarters for COIL's bursting-at-the-seams adult literacy program. And he starts to develop a building for a credit union. "CDCs are good at real estate and business development," Duff says. "Why not help other social service nonprofits do what they do better?"

Veronica Barela. Tough, determined developer of CDC commercial properties in Denver's heavily Hispanic Westside — the same neighborhood where she grew up in one of the city's first public housing projects. She becomes first executive director of the NEWSED CDC, her dream to restore Santa Fe Drive, degenerated into a tawdry downtown commuter artery, to the showcase shopping area it was in the 1940s and 1950s. In 1978 NEWSED's concept paper for a neighborhood-based UDAG project wins a citywide competition; the resulting Alma/Lincoln Park project brings 1,000 housing units, an eleven-story office building, and a major supermarket — not to mention a $1,000 facade-renovation grant for every Westside house. Next comes the handsome Zocalo Shopping Center, bringing eight stores and fifty jobs into the neighborhood. Barela runs into a hornet's nest of political controversy with NEWSED's next endeavor, the Plaza de Santa Fe shopping center — but it is ultimately built and occupied. By 1986 she's attending the Grease Monkey School, under cars, doing lube jobs and changing oil, but also learning franchise

Gary Waldron, a native of the South Bronx and a former IBM executive, shown in one of the greenhouses of GLIE Farms. Explaining how the farms got started, he recalls he "had this crazy idea about agriculture on all that abandoned South Bronx land."

management, soon opening NEWSED's own Grease Monkey on Santa Fe Drive. Admitting it still looks like "pie in the sky," Barela talks of her next vision: bringing to the Westside a mercado, or traditional Hispanic farmer's market.

Sandra Phillips. Firsthand witness to the transformation of a zealous, angry neighborhood, moving from protest to cooperative economic development. Early in the 1970s she leaves a New Jersey teaching position, seeks a master's degree in urban planning from the University of Pittsburgh, settles in Pittsburgh's diverse Oakland section — home turf for the University of Pittsburgh and Carnegie-Mellon, not to mention seven hospitals, museums, and a conservatory. She finds her neighborhood up in arms over the university's plan to gobble up quantities of neighborhood housing, playgrounds, and streets for a major expansion. She joins enraged Oakland residents on the picket lines. Eventually, with city support, they force a community-wide planning process. Boundaries are set to curb university encroachment on residential and commercial land. But it does not stop there. Attention turns to Oakland's central problems — an aging housing stock, traffic congestion, the need for more business diversification. In 1980 the activists form a CDC — the Oakland Planning and Development Corporation. Phillips becomes director; a University of Pittsburgh vice president agrees to sit on the board. Money filters in from the city, the Ford, Mellon Bank, and Howard Heinz foundations, plus a special $610,000 loan fund for CDC projects created by a consortium led by the University of Pittsburgh. Within seven years, the group develops 122 condos and sells them to low-income residents, undertakes the rehab of an abandoned school into more housing, commences to build a major hotel-office complex.

Ruby Duncan helped form Operation Life with other welfare mothers to promote health care and jobs in a depressed Las Vegas neighborhood.

The field directors of the community development movement are as varied in birth and background as all America. They are black, white, Hispanic, Asian, African, American Indian. They are men, and, increasingly, they are women. Quite a few began their careers in the clergy or in government. Some grew up in, then left, then returned to the communities they now seek to revive. Some cut their teeth in the civil rights movement and have been working this field for twenty-five years; others, fresh out of college, law or business school, were toddlers when the Rev. Martin Luther King Jr. stood on the steps of the Lincoln Memorial and proclaimed his dream for a better society. They are former weapons manufacturers, former police officers, former military men and women. They are erstwhile auto workers, missionaries, and welfare mothers. They have been described as "people with a desire to make a difference," as "public entrepreneurs," as society's "anti-bodies," as "warlords retaking ground."

An outsider is struck again and again by their vision, their capacity to look at block upon block of deteriorated or abandoned housing, rural shanties, or boarded-up shops, and, instead of sinking into despair, to see the possibilities of constructive action.

Increasingly, they are practitioners with sophistication and technical capacity. They are people programmed for success, trying to instill that notion in communities where failure is the norm. And so they work incrementally, but seldom if ever passively. In Los Angeles, Terry Watkins chuckles when a visitor asks how big a role her father, Ted Watkins, veteran of the earliest CDC days, continues to play at the Watts Labor Community Action Committee, which he has headed for twenty-two years. "How dominant is father?" she asks rhetorically. "How dominant is Lee Iacocca?"

The leaders of today's CDCs are entrepreneurial and scrappy. They gobble up the few meager resources society makes available, packaging them in ways Rube Goldberg would have found satisfying. Even as they work on nitty-gritty details, they talk of the next "big" project — the sports-medical complex, the farmer's market, the next hundred units of housing, the handsomely renovated commercial strip.

The salaries of these unusual Americans range dramatically, from very low to a fairly competitive $65,000 per year. The hours are long and the frustrations are many. "Private businesses must work with the Catch 22," says Joe Giron, head of Brothers Redevelopment in Denver. "Our deals are even tougher, so I say we work with the Catch 33."

CDCs have indisputably spawned new leadership in American life. Many heads of CDCs have risen to be city council members, mayors, state legislators, and — particularly under the Carter administration — Presidential appointees. The gain has been particularly important among minorities. Arabella Martinez and David B. Carlson, in a study of CDC leadership for Carnegie Corporation, identified several. Henry Cisneros, mayor of San Antonio and former staffer at the Mexican American Unity Council. Wilson Goode, mayor of Philadelphia, who for twelve years directed the Philadelphia Council for Community Advancement, which during his tenure developed, financed, and managed some 2,000 housing units. U.S. Representative Esteban Torres, first director of The East Los Angeles Community Union. And Franklin A. Thomas, president of the Ford Foundation, who was the first president of the Bedford-Stuyvesant Restoration Corporation.

There is some concern among observers of the CDC movement that the future supply of strong CDC leaders, especially in the poorest communities where needs are the greatest, may be choked off by the lack of core budget support from either the federal government or foundations.

The outlook is not entirely bleak, however. Far more so than in earlier days of the movement, talented women appear to be gravitating toward CDC leadership. The proclivity of many women to strive for consensus and seek peaceful resolution of issues could prove a major asset in community organizations where tensions and conflicts are almost endemic.

"Women have been especially successful heading CDCs," notes Ghebre Selassie Mehreteab of the Ford Foundation. "They tend not to be braggarts and to be more pragmatic. We find that the people with capacity to do detailed work, not the super-promoters, are most likely to succeed."

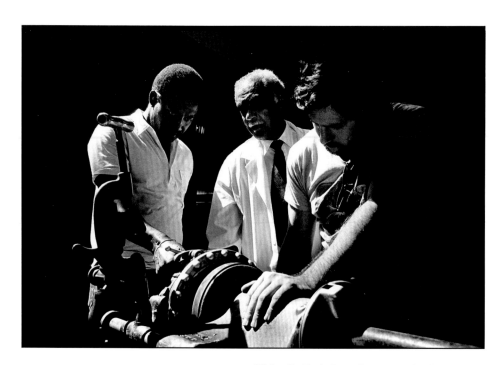

Bidwell Training Center, which retrains unemployed steelworkers, is one of the tenants at 1000 California Avenue, an abandoned warehouse converted into a business incubator by the North Side Civic Development Council in Pittsburgh.

CHAPTER SIX

Where the Money Comes From

1000 California Avenue is a rambling building nearly as long as a football field. It resembles thousands of similar complexes in industrial parks throughout suburban America. But this one is different. First, 1000 California Avenue is smack in the middle of the city of Pittsburgh. Second, it was built — and is owned by — the North Side Civic Development Council, a CDC. And third, it was financed by a scheme so creative and complex that it could serve as a textbook case for a business school curriculum. Complex? Yes. But not all that atypical of the multipartnered projects CDCs are packaging across the United States.

The story begins in the early 1980s, when the Civic Development Council begins to undertake development in Pittsburgh's hilly, meandering North Side neighborhood, best known to outsiders for Three Rivers Stadium, home of the Pittsburgh Steelers and Pirates. Recovery has been slow since the wave of disinvestment in the 1960s. Plenty of abandoned and near-vacant properties remain, among them 1000 California Avenue — formerly a Greyhound bus terminal, then a processing center for the United Parcel Service (UPS). Now it would become the CDC's ambitious first project.

North Side CDC's executive director, Tom Cox, a former clergyman, and its development director, former VISTA volunteer Mark Schneider, seek counsel from Irving Rosenthal, head of Pittsburgh's largest accounting firm. Rosenthal enlists the aid of a contractor friend who builds large surburban industrial parks. They tour the vacant plant and conclude it is ideal for conversion into light industrial bays for small-scale, mostly high-tech tenants. Estimated cost: $2 million.

Step One: Raise a $20,000 "good faith" deposit. UPS wants proof that the CDC's offer to buy the property is serious. Pittsburgh National Bank agrees to loan North Side the money for the deposit. The CDC has six months to raise the $550,000 total purchase price.

Step Two: Seek federal funds. With accountant Rosenthal's help, Cox and Schneider prevail on the Pittsburgh Urban Redevelopment Authority, a city agency, to apply on the CDC's behalf for a $460,000 Urban Development Action Grant from HUD. The city agrees.

Step Three: Solicit loans from the state. The Pennsylvania Industrial Development ment Authority (PIDA) provides very attractive, 3 percent second-mortgage loans for private industrial-park promoters. No neighborhood-based development group has ever applied. PIDA is hesitant. Schneider asks State Representative Tom Murphy, himself a former community organizer, to intercede. After much wrangling, PIDA agrees to lend the CDC $690,000.

Step Four: Go to the banks. Armed with commitments for federal and state funds, Cox and Schneider approach the city's private lenders. The Mellon Bank agrees to a $690,000 mortgage loan and to suspend its requirement that the building be pre-leased.

Step Five: Enlist the foundations. Cox and Schneider want to co-venture the deal with limited private partners. But there's a hitch. The CDC must satisfy an Internal Revenue Service requirement that it have a net worth equal to 15 percent of the equity to be contributed by the partners. It doesn't even come close. The Howard Heinz Endowment, a large local foundation, agrees to give North Side CDC a $75,000 grant to satisfy the IRS.

Step Six: Raise working capital. Before construction can begin, there must be funds to finance pre-closing costs, architectural and legal fees, and survey and marketing expenses. Cox and Schneider turn to the Local Initiatives Support Corporation, which commits a $45,000, two-year loan for working capital.

Step Seven: Bring in the limited partners. Because state PIDA funds are being used in North Side's project, private partners are prohibited from receiving any cash dividends for fifteen years. This is a strong disincentive. So North Side convinces LISC and the city's Urban Redevelopment Authority to contribute $200,000 in bridge financing, which allows the limited partners to stretch out their investments.

September 1984: A fully renovated 1000 California Avenue opens its doors to its first tenants.

September 1986: The building is fully leased, anticipating its first significant profits. All but one occupant is recruited from outside the city. The job generation is solid. The first tenant, Uritec, manufacturer of plastic syringes used by doctors and hospitals, is one of several young firms receiving seed money from the North Side CDC's own venture capital fund.

The North Side Civic Development Council continues its hunt for creative financing and quickly builds an impressive track record. It convinces the state to designate the neighborhood an "enterprise zone" so businesses can qualify for special state incentives. By 1987 the CDC has completed development of a commercial-office complex and a minority-owned retail center. A second light industrial space, Pennsylvania Brighton, is in the works. So is the rehabilitation of the vacant Eberhardt and Oper Brewery, to feature a working brewery as well as incubator space for other small firms. Five homes are rehabbed to test the local residential market. Planning moves ahead for an industrial park on city-owned Herr's Island in the Allegheny River. After investing $10 million to raze old stockyards and slaughterhouses on the island, the city was still unable to entice a private developer. So it asked North Side to take the lead on the project.

Pittsburgh CDCs have enlisted the aid of churches, universities, hospitals, and other local institutions to narrow the gulf between prosperous downtown (seen in the distance) and low-income neighborhoods.

CDCs across the country have shifted into an intensely entrepreneurial mode, whether to finance projects like 1000 California Avenue or to raise urgently needed money for core operating budgets. They are reaching out to local governments, states, churches, foundations, banks, and private corporations, sometimes even to universities and hospitals. The new alliances are CDCs' sole road to survival and growth as federal support of community development continues to shrink. Indeed, it is nearly impossible to find one CDC among the thousands that does not now feature some form of partnership financing.

A paradigm of the times is Eastside Community Investments (ECI), a highly successful ten-year-old CDC in Indianapolis. In 1980 almost 90 percent of its $506,752 budget came from the federal government — $440,129 from the Community Services Administration, $30,000 from Community Development Block Grant (CDBG) pass-throughs from the city. By 1986 ECI's operating revenues had been sliced in half, to $271,800. Only 16 percent of that came from Uncle Sam (some $43,000 in CDBG funds). In spite of cuts so deep they would likely sink any private business, ECI has continued to pull off an impressive string of major projects, assisting in the rehab of 1,000 units of housing, starting a housing-weatherization program, a below-market mortgage pool, a small-business incubator and technical assistance program, and developing a twenty-five-acre industrial park, bringing in 300 jobs.

How did ECI adapt? "The cuts forced us to utilize our own resources better and extend our network," says ECI President Dennis West. The CDC pared staff, dropped some programs, and shifted some activities to for-profit subsidiaries. But mostly, "we turned to the larger community," West explains. "We found that when we approached people in a personal way, for investments, resources, or volunteers, they would respond."

Indeed they have. ECI's 1986 annual report lists nearly 100 "partners" that have supplied financing, *pro bono publico* assistance and technical exper-tise for a dozen of its projects. Among the multiple partners: the city, the state, the federal government, Indiana Power and Light, the Joyce Foundation, the Lilly Endowment, four church organizations, Goodwill Industries, Aetna Life and Casualty, half a dozen banks and realtors, LISC, the Indiana School for the Deaf, accounting firms, law firms, and McDonald's.

Raising money for CDC activities in today's environment is difficult, time-consuming, draining. But some believe the emerging new relationships are expanding CDCs' potential impact light-years beyond earlier days when their contact was generally confined to federal funders and a few leading foundations or churches.

"The partnership concept is opening up a whole new vein of relationships," notes Renee Berger, a leading national expert on the new generation of public-private initiatives. "We are seeing, in fact, a dramatic new melding of the sectors for problem solving."

"The interplay between people is mold-breaking," adds Paul Grogan, president of LISC. "You find that community leaders are sophisticated and talented, government leaders entrepreneurial, and bankers have hearts and care about social problems."

ECI's Dennis West concurs. "Our CDC has given the wider community an institutional point of reference to connect with the poor," he says. "In the long run, that may be the only way to affect real changes."

But West and other CDC leaders warn that the new partnerships are still embryonic, and are developing very unevenly across the country. To reach their fullest potential, the new partnerships urgently need stronger public reinforcement and support.

"Real creativity is occurring in the neighborhoods of this country," West notes. "We must have governmental resources — federal, state, and local — to help respond to those initiatives."

"The rhetoric of private-sector initiatives is wearing a little thin," adds Richard Fleming, president of the Denver Chamber of Commerce. "Corporations are getting outraged as the federal government withdraws from one area after another. We need a larger vision. We're not a bunch of Balkan states."

"We've barely scratched the surface in attracting new public and private institutional support to CDCs," says Paul Grogan. "If we don't do more, I'm afraid CDCs will become a colorful but minor footnote to U.S. social and economic development in the late twentieth century."

FEDERAL GOVERNMENT SUPPORT

Many CDC supporters look longingly to "the good old days" of the 1960s and 1970s, when federal support for neighborhood-based development, though largely uncoordinated and widely scattered among the agencies, was considered relatively generous. By the end of the Carter administration, according to a study by Alan J. Abramson and Lester M. Salamon of the Urban Institute, an estimated $2.6 billion in federal funds was flowing each year to community development projects through a panoply of programs. By 1985 federal commitments had dropped to $1.6 billion in inflation-adjusted dollars; for fiscal year 1987 the Reagan budget proposed a further cut to $1.1 billion.

During the same six years when federal resources were cut in half, however, the number of CDCs doubled. One result: fierce competition for remaining federal money. "It's a real crap shoot," says ECI's Dennis West.

"The odds are so heavily stacked against you. We don't approach any project thinking we'll get federal dollars."

With the demise in 1981 of the Community Services Administration, CDCs lost virtually all direct federal support for technical assistance, staff salaries, core budget operations, and administrative costs. Previously, CSA had been supplying such funding to the tune of $30 million to $40 million annually.

Many CDCs do continue to collect federal dollars to help finance specific projects. These project funds come directly to CDCs from the Economic Development Administration or from the Secretary's Discretionary Fund in the Department of Health and Human Services' Office of Community Services. Some CDCs have followed North Side's example in Pittsburgh and prevailed on supportive local governments to win Urban Development Action Grants from HUD. A substantial number of CDCs receive some Community Development Block Grant funds channeled through their city halls, both for projects and core operations.

Other minor sources of federal funding for CDC projects include HUD's Section 202 subsidies for housing construction for the elderly and a small HUD-administered Neighborhood Development Demonstration program. A handful of CDCs have entered into service-delivery contracts with various federal departments and agencies, including Health and Human Services, the Small Business Administration, and the Department of Labor. One example: managing programs under the Jobs Training Partnership Act.

How much do CDCs now need government support? How successful can they be without it?

Those who know the movement best say some subsidy is essential. CDCs operate in neighborhoods where the free market failed in the first instance. Even if a CDC proves adept at assembling financing packages so imaginative they'd be the envy of any mortgage banker, that doesn't mean it is truly self-sufficient. "We cannot pretend market forces are going to revive these communities," says LISC president Paul Grogan. "The subsidy has to come from somewhere."

It was precisely because the United States lacked a sustained national development policy that indigenous local efforts sprang up — in the words of Pratt Institute's Ron Schiffman — "to combat enormous social, economic, and physical problems that result from poverty and inequality." But those local efforts, he warns, may be "doomed to continuous cycles of frustration" in the absence of a supportive national policy, including financial support.

As the Reagan era draws to a close, CDC advocates suggest that the time may be ripe for a renewed and broadened public support of the movement. Among some, there is hope that the pendulum of national policy has gone as far right as it will and that in a coming leftward swing there will be renewed federal funding. CDCs, it is thought, might benefit from rediscovered national interest in welfare and poverty problems. Chances for expanded federal funding of community development remain clouded, however, by the continuation of towering national deficits.

On a parallel track there is belief that community development organizations have proven so successful, as Andrew Mott of the Center for Community Change notes, that they will "sooner or later be seized upon as a central element of public policy." The growing ranks of influential state and local officials expounding the benefits of community-based development increase the chances of greater national attention. Among governors, Massachusetts' Michael Dukakis, a Democrat, is perhaps the most celebrated proponent. But the ranks of mayors prominently identified with the same approach is clearly bipartisan, ranging from Republicans George Voinovich of Cleveland and William Hudnut of Indianapolis to Democrats Raymond Flynn of Boston, Wilson Goode of Philadelphia, Xavier Suarez of Miami, and Richard Caliguiri of Pittsburgh. Among the first Presidential contenders to talk of the potential of community-based groups was conservative Republican Congressman Jack Kemp of New York.

Even without major grant funds, CDC backers believe the federal government could be far more supportive. Joseph McNeely of the Development Training Institute suggests that the federal government "can play a gigantic role in knowledge development, technical transfer, assistance for networking of community people, and conferences to exchange information."

STATE AND LOCAL GOVERNMENT SUPPORT

The CDCs' most important new support base may turn out to be state governments, both because of federal fiscal limits and because some states are starting to see community development as an element of their overall economic development and antipoverty efforts.

Leader of the band among the states backing CDCs is Massachusetts. That interest has roots going back to the early 1970s when State Representative Mel King, a prominent Boston politician, set up a "Wednesday Morning Group" of community activists, academics, and state legislators. The group designed and secured approval of a state Community Development Finance Corporation, which provides small loans and venture capital to CDCs for housing and other projects. (A $10 million general obligation state bond, passed in 1977, provides its major funding.) Next came the Community Economic Development and Assistance Corporation (CEDAC), which provides technical assistance and small, interest-free loans to help CDCs get their projects started. CEDAC initially tried to support CDCs in major business ventures, but got its fingers burned in several failures; it now concentrates almost exclusively on real estate and low-income housing.

Finally, Massachusetts in 1978 created the Community Enterprise Economic Development (CEED) program, a linchpin because it provides about half the state's seventy CDCs with yearly grants for core budgets. The dollars per organization are not huge — about $28,000 annually for staff and operations — but the funding is competitive, which tends to keep the CDCs on their toes. Funding by FY 1987 had reached $1.3 million as CEED made an aggressive effort to cover all economically distressed parts of the state.

No state matches Massachusetts' alphabet soup of economic development agencies, including those targeted on CDCs. But by 1987 statewide CDC networks had been organized in some nine states. In New York, Minnesota, Wisconsin, Florida, and Ohio, CDCs had secured state funding.

Cities have become the final — and potentially most critical — partner of CDCs. (The contrast with the 1960s could not be more vivid; then federally funded community action programs operated without the blessing of, and frequently clashed with, city halls.)

"The atmosphere has changed across the United States," says Denver's Mayor Federico Pena. "City governments are opening their doors. If you're a community activist and do your nuts-and-bolts work, you'll get a response from the city." With federal aid cutbacks, Pena said, "we'd be foolish not to find alternative funds from city coffers to make CDC projects work. They're a wise investment for the future of the city."

One can find cities indifferent to their CDCs. But the trend is toward active cooperation and support. More and more cities are providing access to city community development officials; some cities have a specifically designated coordination officer. Efforts are being made to streamline permit processes for CDC projects. Some cities provide technical assistance. Others enter into direct partnerships with CDCs, often in conjunction with LISC, Ford, or local foundations and corporations.

A handful of cities have gone much farther. Boston, Cleveland, and New York are among those that have made CDCs and allied nonprofits prime suppliers of new and renovated low-income housing. The city of Philadelphia is cooperating with CDCs in "landbanking" tax-delinquent and abandoned properties, mostly residential, until the CDCs can mobilize restoration programs. Pittsburgh has earmarked repayments from federal UDAG loans made to private developers — some $400,000 per year — for grants of up to $75,000 to help CDCs initiate development projects.

CDCs in some cities are also beginning to benefit from so-called "linkage" schemes — the requirement that major private developers, in return for zoning clearances or permits, contribute to low-income housing and other social programs. Boston Mayor Ray Flynn claims "the philosophy is simple: We have to be sure the growth of downtown is shared with people who have traditionally been left behind." In what must be the nation's most audacious effort, Boston has linked the development of a choice downtown parcel, owned by the city, with a potential office complex on several acres of barren land, cleared for a highway never built, in the predominantly black Roxbury section. The developer of the downtown site must put up the building in Roxbury, which will have "back-office" space for major firms, providing a rich source of local employment. The developer must also share 25 percent of the ownership of both projects with CDCs and other minority owners. San Francisco, Miami, Seattle, Hartford, and Washington, D.C., are among other cities that are using linkage to raise funds for community development.

THE FOUNDATIONS

From the earliest days of CDCs, foundations have played a critical role. The Ford Foundation is widely regarded as the philanthropic pacesetter. Its pioneering Gray Areas program of the early 1960s eventually became the model for the nationwide "community action agencies" of the Johnsonian era's Great Society. By the early 1970s Ford was supporting nine first-generation CDCs, spread geographically from Bedford-Stuyvesant to the Mississippi Delta to Watts.

Over two decades, Ford has committed some $170 million in grants and loans to CDCs, the largest amount of any foundation. Ford also funds a wide array of national and local organizations supplying technical assistance to CDCs. In 1977 Ford officers conceived the idea of an experimental "bank" to provide more substantial financing assistance to CDCs. That "bank" became the Local Initiatives Support Corporation, which was launched in 1980 with $4.75 million from Ford, matched by an equal amount from six corporations. Ford was also a pioneer in using "program-related investments" (PRIs), drawn from its capital assets, to supply equity and low-interest loans to risky commercial and nonprofit enterprises. By 1986 Ford's PRIs consisted of $14 million in new commitments annually, and had reached a total of some $70 million. The major share went to support CDC activities directly or through such financial intermediaries as LISC, the Enterprise Foundation, the Institute for Community Economics, and the Inner City Ventures Fund of the National Trust for Historic Preservation.

In 1982 Ford opened another chapter in CDC funding with a new grant program aimed specifically at "emerging" CDCs — not the more experienced organizations the foundation had long supported, but newer "adolescent" groups struggling to get on their feet. The object was to permit the new groups to hire high-caliber staff at competitive salaries, and to attract support from private lenders and funders as well. Within four years the foundation had provided some $30 million in grants and loans to three dozen

CDCs in twenty cities. More than half the grants were being funneled through what might be called "philanthropic federalism" — Ford backing in partnership with local governments and foundations. Instead of the familiar direct Ford-to-CDC relationship, says Bernard McDonald, head of Ford's Urban Poverty program, the Foundation was "deliberately building a cooperative approach." Local foundations and city governments were not only invited to share in funding projects but also given a major role in filtering applications. Ford's chief goals, says McDonald, were "to stretch limited dollars and assure ongoing local support when a national foundation withdraws."

By 1987 Ford's philanthropic partnerships had spread to six cities — Pittsburgh, Philadelphia, Denver, Washington, Baltimore, and Cleveland. In Pittsburgh, its local partners included city hall and the Heinz and Mellon foundations, targeting five neighborhoods. In Denver, Ford teamed up with the city, the Colorado Housing and Finance Authority (a state agency), and the Piton Foundation, a major local funder of community development, to create a new $5 million pool for CDCs. In Philadelphia, six CDCs were receiving core support from a collaborative that included Ford, the Pew Memorial Trust, and the city. And in Cleveland, Ford's partners were the city government, Standard Oil Co. (Ohio), and the Cleveland and George Gund foundations.

A comprehensive list of other private foundations supporting CDCs is beyond the scope of this study. Those particularly active in the field include the Charles Stewart Mott Foundation, Levi Strauss, ARCO Foundation, the McKnight Foundation, Standard Oil, the Lilly Endowment, the Joyce Foundation, the Northwest Area Foundation, Honeywell Foundation, Dayton-Hudson Foundation, the Hewlett Foundation, the Mary Reynolds Babcock Foundation, and the MacArthur Foundation.

In recent years the CDC movement has made some inroads in winning new philanthropic resources. But as the 1980s draw to a close, community development still ranks light-years behind such traditional foundation causes as education, health and human services, cultural activities, and United Way. (The huge United Way network, observers note, has with a few exceptions largely shied away from funding CDC economic development projects.)

To remedy the situation, in 1986 a new private funders "affinity" group was formed. The Task Force on Community Economic Development was charged with devising an aggressive strategy to increase philanthropic support for CDCs. According to Chairman Lance Buhl, manager of contributions for Standard Oil (Ohio): "The financial commitments by all American philanthropy total more than $70 billion a year. We would be lucky to find $1 billion earmarked for community economic development."

A public housing playground in Watts, Los Angeles. Flaws in the urban renewal of the 1950s and in the "war on poverty" of the 1960s convinced CDC leaders to try something new. Most CDCs now combine social and economic programs to raise incomes, create jobs, generate community-run enterprises, and attract businesses to their neighborhoods.

The problem, Buhl explains, is that many philanthropies are simply uninformed about CDC activities or still think of them as the strident advocates of the 1960s. He notes that some funders don't see community development as "charitable," or they remain skeptical of projects already funded. Richard Steckel, a business consultant who markets nonprofit causes, elucidates: "Economic development is just not warm and fuzzy. It's not easy to sell."

Competition from other worthy causes remains the biggest single problem. Council on Foundations President James A. Joseph sums up the dilemma: "Foundations face a queue of desperate organizations, and we dole out the funds until they are exhausted, leaving most organizations in line with nothing. We try to compensate for this inherent unfairness by rotating the organizations that are at the head of the line every year."

Another problem, notes Pablo Eisenberg of the Center for Community Change, is that foundations are reluctant to abandon longstanding priorities and causes, even though national needs have changed.

One beacon of hope for CDC forces may be the panoply of new community foundations proliferating rapidly around the country, from fewer than 200 in 1975 to 317 in 1986, with collective assets grown to more than $3.5 billion. Sometimes referred to as "public charities," these nontraditional philanthropies raise most of their funds from local sources and most give within their own geographic area. Community foundations can today be found in large cities from Atlanta to Boston to Chicago to San Francisco, as well as in numerous smaller cities. Quite a few have elevated community development to a higher priority in their contribution plans.

But perhaps none among the hundreds could justifiably claim to be more supportive of CDC activities than the Cleveland Foundation, the nation's first community foundation, founded in 1914. Among cities, Cleveland has an unusually strong and diverse network of neighborhood-based organizations; today it would be hard to find many significant community development activities in the city that had not received Cleveland Foundation backing. Among the CDCs on its long list were: Famicos Foundation, prolific nonprofit housing developer and a major partner in Lexington Village, a 600-unit apartment and town-house complex in Hough, hard hit in the riots of the 1960s (the extraordinary public-private partnership behind that project helped win for Cleveland an "All America Cities" award in 1985, its third in five years); Union-Miles Development Corporation, fighting abandonment in southeast Cleveland; and the Detroit-Shoreway Community Development Organization, a feisty fourteen-year-old CDC promoting housing and commercial redevelopment on Cleveland's west side. (Detroit-Shoreway's longtime executive director, Raymond Pianka, was recently elected to the Cleveland City Council.)

The Cleveland Foundation has also extended its largesse to a host of other organizations supporting housing and community development, ranging from the Center for Neighborhood Development at Cleveland State University to the Cleveland Housing Network, an innovative umbrella organization of nonprofit housing developers that has been a pioneer in dramatically reducing housing rehabilitation costs.

RELIGIOUS-BASED SUPPORT

Like foundations, religious congregations have been an integral part of the CDC movement from its outset. Literally dozens of CDCs began in church basements. Regional and national religious councils, led by such organizations as the Catholic Church's Campaign for Human Development and the Presbyterian Self Development of Peoples Fund, have committed millions of dollars of financial support for organizing and projects. Thousands of local congregations, including some affluent suburban churches and synagogues, have contributed staff services, volunteers, meeting space, and equipment, or prevailed on their members to fill collection plates for community programs and projects.

The greatest asset religious groups bring to the CDC movement may be their almost universal presence, penetrating nearly every nook and cranny of American communities. Congregations have become especially important community development building blocks in underclass neighborhoods, where traditional bastions of organizing — the unions, ethnic associations, and political clubs — have fled along with middle-class residents.

Far more than government or foundations, religious institutions are more likely to assume the risk of supporting advocacy groups or fledgling development organizations until they can grow to a significant presence. For many groups in the early stages of development, church identification provides crucial legitimization. And the clergy often provide important brokering services with public officials and funders.

"One can't treat churches like foundations," says Louis Knowles, director of religious philanthropy for the Council on Foundations. "Churches don't think of themselves as grant makers. They think of themselves as living institutions that want to be involved in neighborhoods."

The national network of religious-based support for CDCs is ecumenical and diverse. Groups range from newcomers, such as the Jewish Fund for Justice, to longstanding, pioneering institutions such as the Campaign for Human Development (CHD) of the U.S. Catholic Conference. Since 1970 CHD has provided more than $100 million in grants and interest-free loans to some 2,500 self-help projects. (Local CHD committees, about 140 in number, have contributed millions more to projects in their communities.) The

National Congress of Black Churches has been a seminal source of networking and resources for community development efforts in many minority communities. Evangelical Christian churches, too, have established their own network — World Vision — to support development efforts of the poor. There is also a national organization promoting community investments by religious groups — the New York-based Interfaith Center on Corporate Responsibility.

Local churches have taken on a major, and dramatic, role in Brooklyn, N.Y., through the Industrial Areas Foundation (IAF), fathered by the late community organizer Saul Alinsky. Alinsky and his colleagues, including Ed Chambers, now IAF's executive director, determined that churches were the only strong, viable institution capable of community organization in the nation's barrios and ghettos. Development was not and is still not IAF's principal interest. "We're much more interested in process than in program, in empowering people," Chambers explains. IAF leaders in fact show some disdain for CDCs, which they believe become enmeshed in the details of development and fail to provide a significant organizing tool among the nation's poor.

But the results in development terms, especially housing, have sometimes been impressive. IAF's biggest claimed achievement is the Nehemiah Plan, which first built several hundred row houses in Brooklyn's Brownsville section and by late 1986 had a city-approved plan for 1,100 more units and a third phase with some 3,000 units on the drawing boards. The effort began when five pastors from Brooklyn churches — Roman Catholic, Baptist, and Lutheran — invited IAF to form a local social action group. The result was the East Brooklyn Churches organization, a coalition of fifty-two local congregations that has over 30,000 members and also claims major success in voter registration. The inspiration for the housing came from I.D. Robbins, a retired builder, civic activist, and onetime mayoral candidate who ran the construction program. The group organized an $8 million financing pool, with the largest contributions from the Missouri Synod of the Lutheran Church ($1 million), the Catholic Diocese of Brooklyn ($3 million), and the Episcopal Diocese of Long Island ($1 million).

East Brooklyn Churches then went after a major commitment from the New York City government, getting the attention of Mayor Edward Koch by sending a delegation led by Roman Catholic Bishop Francis J. Mugavero. The result: a $10 million city fund that made it possible to cut $10,000 off the price of each unit built. The city also agreed to donate the land, which it had claimed through tax default. The State of New York's Mortgage Agency agreed to provide mortgages at interest below the market rate. Many of the new homeowners, primarily black and Hispanic, had been living in public housing.

PRIVATE CORPORATIONS AND BANKS

Corporate and banking America has become a major partner in hundreds of CDC activities and projects. The evidence is in from all across the country, from the Tacolcy CDC's Edison Plaza in Miami to the Cross Town Industrial Park in Boston, from the Chicago Equity Fund, which is providing millions in private financing for CDC-built housing in Chicago, to the Bank of America's $10 million no-interest loan to the Local Initiatives Support Corporation. This stands in stark contrast to the turbulent 1960s, when community groups and corporations so often found themselves at loggerheads, when private companies by the thousands were abandoning urban neighborhoods for the more hospitable environs of the suburbs.

A 1986 survey by The Conference Board documents a near-doubling of corporate contributions to community development since 1975. In the subcategory of housing, corporate gifts have multiplied nearly 500 percent.

Nor does outright giving tell the whole story. Even more significant has been the increased willingness of the private sector to participate in CDC projects as "investors" and partners. Particularly notable is the nation's insurance industry — led by such companies as Aetna Life and Casualty, Prudential Insurance Company, CIGNA, and the Equitable Assurance Society. Beginning in the late 1960s, in response to urban rioting, insurance companies set an industry-wide goal of investing some $2 billion in low- and moderate-income housing, job creation, and improved social services for inner-city residents. The industry later went on to establish its own organization to promote social investing — the Center for Corporate Public Involvement. In addition to investing in CDC projects, the insurance industry has been a major investor in many partnerships organized by Neighborhood Housing Services throughout the country.

Some corporations have made the ultimate investment — locating a major plant in a job-starved CDC area. The pioneer was IBM in the 1960s; its Bed-Stuy plant today employs 400 workers. More recent examples include Digital Equipment Corporation, which constructed a new, 250-employee plant in an industrial park in Boston's Roxbury neighborhood (the park itself was established largely through the efforts of the Community Development Corporation of Boston); and American Cablevision, which today employs 200 people in an industrial park developed by Eastside Community Investments, an Indianapolis CDC. In addition, hundreds of major retail and food chains — from Payless Shoes to McDonald's — pay rents to CDCs as tenants of CDC-built shopping and commercial centers.

There are even instances of corporations creating their own CDCs. A prime example: Tasty Baking Co., which in 1968 established the Allegheny West Foundation to stabilize its declining North Philadelphia neighborhood. Over the years, Allegheny West's multiple projects have included housing rehabilitation, community gardens, commercial redevelopment, and job placement for teenagers.

As for the nation's banks, they vary dramatically in their willingness to support CDC projects. In an industry known for its conservatism, it is not uncommon for CDC managers to approach numerous financial institutions before finding one that will lend to a CDC project. But there are also quite a few banks that have actively supported CDC efforts for years, extending millions of dollars in credit to local projects or contributing to national CDC intermediaries such as LISC and the Enterprise Foundation. Some banks, too, are stepping up their community lending as a result of the federal Community Reinvestment Act (CRA), which has given community organizations a potent new tool to challenge banks' community lending records. By 1987 community coalitions in more than 100 cities and towns had negotiated major CRA agreements with local banks, thus generating more capital for credit-starved neighborhoods.

Perhaps no bank could claim a stronger commitment to community revitalization — or more dramatic results — than the South Shore Bank in Chicago. A visitor to South Shore, in one of those neighborhoods that turned from white to black after the racial upheavals of the 1960s, sees nothing all that exceptional. There are healthy lines of depositors on the first floor, along with plants, art work, tasteful decor. Upstairs are the mortgage and commercial lending departments, and the offices of the bank holding company, Shorebank Corp. (formerly Illinois Neighborhood Development Corp.).

But probe South Shore's history and a unique story emerges. It begins with Ron Grzywinski, businessman and pioneer in community-oriented banking, who bought the bank in 1973 after federal regulators had refused to allow the former owners to pull the bank out of the neighborhood altogether. Grzywinski's intent was (and remains) to operate a profitable banking operation. But he and his colleagues had broader goals: to leapfrog the redlining phenomenon of those times and provide credit for South Shore families and businesses that needed it, to demonstrate that a commercial bank can be profitable in a black neighborhood, to serve as a catalyst for community revitalization.

A decade and a half later, the bank's assets had climbed from $40 million to $135 million and it was registering annual profits of over $1 million. More than $140 million had been invested in the South Shore neighborhood through the bank and the other operations of the holding company. Indeed, Shorebank had financed rehabilitation of more than 8,000 units — one-quarter of all the housing stock in the neighborhood.

To do that Grzywinski devised a number of mechanisms appropriate for a lower-income neighborhood. Utilizing the holding company as an umbrella, he established affiliates that include, in addition to the bank itself: (1) the Neighborhood Fund, a minority enterprise investment corporation (MESBIC), licensed by the Small Business Administration, to make equity capital and loan investments; (2) City Lands Corporation, which handles larger buildings in need of rehabilitation and has developed a shopping center; and (3) the Neighborhood Institute, focusing on housing and job programs for the South Shore's poorest residents.

In addition to regular local deposits, the bank by 1987 had attracted some $50 million in deposits from socially oriented investors across the United States and even abroad. It had also raised $3 million through its innovative "rehab CD" (certificate of deposit) program: investors agree to give up a portion of their regular interest payments and that money goes into the bank's special investment fund for housing. The fund helps write down the borrowing costs for rehabilitation so that developers can charge less than market rates for rentals.

Says bank chairman Milton Davis: "Most CDCs raise a pot of money, spend it, and that's it. Here we're taking ordinary insured bank deposits and putting them to work for redevelopment. It can keep going on and on and on."

Sixth Street Marketplace in Richmond, Va., built by a subsidiary of the Enterprise Foundation. The foundation is one of several intermediary organizations that provide CDCs with financing and technical assistance, and help obtain corporate and government support for CDC activities.

CHAPTER SEVEN

The Networkers

After suffering the whirlwind of racial upheaval in the 1960s and the cataclysmic disinvestment of the 1970s, Chicago's West Garfield Park strives to regain stability, to provide residents with the rudiments of safety and opportunity that middle-class neighborhoods enjoy. The 1960s saw 37,000 whites leave, 40,000 blacks move in; now the neighborhood is 97 percent black, largely poor. By the early 1980s, 5,000 housing units had disappeared, victims of tenant abuse and landlord neglect. Vacant lots are everywhere. The deteriorated Madison Avenue commercial strip is filled with cheap five-and-dime stores and bars, most of them operated by Koreans and other immigrants.

Enter, in 1979, Bethel New Life, a CDC sparked by the neighborhood's Lutheran Church and a feisty former missionary to Africa, Mary Nelson. By 1987 Bethel has brought on line 371 housing units — apartments, town houses, sweat-equity co-ops. One building, the Living-Learning Center in a once-abandoned public school, has twenty-six low-income apartments upstairs and the Bethel Christian School below.

Bethel New Life expands to a 150-person payroll. Eighty work in a program for seniors financed through city and state contracts. Twenty are in Bethel's Wholistic Health Center, providing full medical services for 800 patients a month, plus information on such matters as contraception, nutrition, and alcoholism. Eight, including an architect, are on Bethel's construction crews, ten on the property management staff. Three run Bethel's "cash for trash" recycling center, a way for local scavengers — Mary Nelson calls them "alley entrepreneurs" — to take in some $140,000 a year for glass, metals, and newspapers. Other staffers work in a sewing cooperative, job-placement center, or programs that range from cooking classes to counseling for homeowners.

Where does Bethel New Life's money come from? From foundations large and small, with AMOCO, First National Bank of Chicago, MacArthur, Kellogg, Joyce, and Harris Bank foundations prominent on the roster. From churches — predictably the national Lutheran Church, but also the Catholic Church's Campaign for Human Development and the Evangelicals' World Vision. From government and a long list of private contributors. Habitat for Humanity, a national housing group, builds homes with Bethel New Life. For one week in summer 1986 a Habitat-Bethel project brings in Jimmy, Rosalynn, and Amy Carter, not to mention Chuck Colson (former communications director in the Nixon White House), six prisoners, and eighty other volunteers, to rehabilitate four West Garfield homes. Uncommonly among CDCs, Bethel New Life also receives funds as a United Way member agency.

"Networking" could well be Bethel New Life's middle name. The Local Initiatives Support Corporation makes three major loans for Bethel housing projects. The Enterprise Foundation becomes a partner in four. The Chicago Equity Fund helps in three. And Bethel figures prominently in dozens of Chicago community alliances and coalitions.

Says Mary Nelson: "I believe we're just about to the point where we're going to tip this neighborhood for the positive. On the corridor where we've focused our greatest efforts you see flowers, picket fences, green gardens — like the suburbs. In a year, we probably touch 10,000 of the 40,000 people in our community."

The very name of the Peoples Involvement Corporation of Washington, D.C., suggests its roots in the "antipoverty" era of the late 1960s. Yet as executive director Andree Gandy quickly tells a visitor, PIC has come leagues since then. A broad array of social services continues — food banks and welfare referral now augmented by job fairs and a word-processing training center. Because of constituent needs PIC could hardly do otherwise; its territory includes not only the infamous 14th Street corridor destroyed in the 1968 riots but much of Shaw and the environs of Howard University, among the city's lowest-income, most depressed neighborhoods.

But there is an economic development side to PIC in the 1980s. It has begun several housing developments. And now, at a critical neighborhood intersection on the verge of getting a Metro station, PIC has taken effective control of the real estate on three of four corners. It is erecting a drug store, co-venturing with a church a mixed-use office building, and planning a farmer's market and restaurant in the old Dunbar Theater. Now Gandy speaks with excitement of an even greater opportunity — Howard Plaza, a joint partnership with Howard University to develop Washington's own version of Harvard Square: acres of student-oriented stores, restaurants, theaters, and housing.

Predevelopment costs have been covered in large measure by recoverable grants from LISC. And when Gandy decided her development skills needed sharpening, she spent a year in the intensive training program for CDC managers run by the Baltimore-based Development Training Institute.

A Denver CDC is building this auto repair shop, which will employ local residents. The CDC also offers training in how to manage repair-shop franchises.

Like hundreds of their sister CDCs across the country, Bethel New Life and the Peoples Involvement Corporation are getting critical assistance from a new infrastructure of national and local CDC support organizations. They go by the dull name of "intermediaries"; in fact they are extraordinarily helpful networkers for the burgeoning CDC movement. They provide new financing streams, advanced technical assistance, a means of coordinating CDC activities that the pioneer CDCs never had at their disposal. Intermediaries have become particularly consequential in brokering new corporate and local government support for CDCs. They have become the best means of cross-pollinating successful models. Politically, the intermediaries claim no small role in winning new tax credits for low-income housing in the 1986 Tax Reform Act. Their success, some say, may be the harbinger of a brand-new CDC force at the national level.

By and large, the emergence of the intermediaries is a 1980s phenomenon — even though some have roots going back to the 1960s. And although such national intermediaries as LISC receive most of the attention, local intermediaries have grown rapidly, packaging financing, administering, and coordinating the burgeoning variety of public-private community development and housing partnerships.

"Intermediaries represent the kind of expertise with which private-sector representatives are comfortable and used to dealing," says the New World Foundation in a 1980 study of neighborhood initiatives. "With broad credibility and knowledge of significant portions of the community self-help world, intermediaries are in a unique position to bridge the gaps between the sectors," the report continues.

What constitutes an intermediary? They are infinitely varied. Intermediaries provide everything from financing and deal packaging to legal advice, contacts, and moral support. They range from well-staffed national professional organizations to one or two people in a local foundation or in city hall. Some have a private-sector orientation; others reflect the organizing and advocacy mode of the 1960s. Sometimes, more mature CDCs themselves act as intermediaries, helping newer groups get their staffs, funding, and projects up to speed.

"The base is not as important as the role," says Andrew Mott of the Center for Community Change. "The good intermediaries create an environment which nurtures the growth of vital organizations; they devote time and skill to watching for the seeds of new organizations, help emerging groups get through their first few months and first crisis, assist in raising the crucial early money, connect people with others who have relevant experience, and help them find and break in their initial staff. One particular value is an ability to bring groups together to work in coalitions on larger issues or projects."

LOCAL INITIATIVES SUPPORT CORPORATION

According to one version of the story, the idea of LISC was born in 1977 on an Amtrak train transporting the Ford Foundation's Board of Trustees back to New York after a tour of Baltimore neighborhood projects. One trustee asked Ford Vice President Mitchell Sviridoff what he would do with $25 million for neighborhood development. In the ensuing discussions, on the train and later back at Ford, the idea gradually took shape for a new "bank" that would supply grants and loans to CDCs, demand from them hard-nosed business accountability, and leverage additional CDC investments from local businesses, foundations, and government. LISC was established a couple of years later; Sviridoff left Ford to become LISC's founding president.

Today LISC claims to be the largest private, nonprofit community development organization in the country. Beginning with less than $10 million in 1980 (raised from Ford and six corporations), LISC had grown to over $130 million in 1987.

The LISC-Ford connection remains a close one. About one-fourth of LISC's total funding has come from Ford — more than $34 million, including $7.1 million committed in late 1986. The remaining millions have come from 375 investors and contributors that read like a "Who's Who" of American business and philanthropy — dozens of major corporations, insurance companies, banks, utilities, and media conglomerates.

From an initial handful of community organizations, LISC had by mid-1987 made more than 700 grants and loans to 408 groups in 119 cities and towns. Its investments had triggered $580 million for CDC projects from other sources. All told, LISC claims to have financed over 10,000 units of housing and 2.6 million square feet of commercial and industrial real estate.

One important element of the LISC strategy is to target "areas of concentration" to enhance the scale of CDC activities in selected cities and states. LISC in effect challenges local business and philanthropic establishments to come up with a funding commitment to match LISC's own for that area. The local advisory committee then recommends projects for LISC funding. By 1986 twenty-three cities, two regions, and two states had been chosen, including Baltimore, Boston, Chicago, Cincinnati, Cleveland, Denver, East St. Louis, Indianapolis, Houston, Miami, Newark, Norfolk, Omaha, Seattle, the Monongahela Valley of Pennsylvania, and eastern North Carolina.

LISC's California network, one of its first, is especially well-developed. It had by 1986 made seventy-nine loans and grants, worth nearly $8 million, to forty-one CDCs in twenty-four California cities, leveraging an additional $30 million from public and private sources. Among the wide range of LISC-supported groups: the Los Angeles Community Design Center, which packages real estate deals for nonprofits and has developed eleven mobilehome cooperatives; the Skid Row Development Corporation, a Los Angeles CDC that creates businesses and housing for the homeless; and the Tenderloin Neighborhood Development Corporation in San Francisco, developer of a residential hotel.

The CDCs receiving LISC support are expected to take a bottom-line approach and to strengthen their own management capabilities, assets, and income. Deals are structured so as to bring local banks and other private lenders and investors into each project. On average, LISC funds account for only about 10 percent of a project's cost.

Says Peter Goldmark, a vice-president of the Times Mirror Company and a member of the LISC Board: "LISC deals are a curious blend of social investment and business discipline. LISC builds the capacity of CDCs to structure their deals in business terms, and that makes corporations and bankers comfortable. The lender has the satisfaction of making a loan, getting repaid, and contributing to the community at the same time. LISC-sponsored deals provide a systematic way of linking corporate capital to neighborhood rebuilding. It's a public policy success story."

Explains Paul Grogan, who succeeded Sviridoff as LISC president in 1986: "LISC's role is to act as agent provocateur. First we acquaint the local business community with CDCs and get them excited, through neighborhood tours, presentations, and the like. Then we approach the various local institutional players — the banks, businesses, city and state governments — with specific ideas about how they could participate in a scaled-up program. It's customized by city. We try to translate a general new enthusiasm into a distinct set of requests that emanate from a plan on how you do so many housing units or a commercial project. Frequently it helps to have the local community establish a goal."

LISC-supported projects range dramatically, and may include anything from modest grants for CDC staff development to small loans for housing rehab to grander efforts such as the Boston and Chicago housing partnerships. It's not uncommon to find LISC participation in major CDC commercial ventures, particularly in the crucial early stages. Examples: the Tacolcy CDC's Edison Plaza in Miami and 1000 California Avenue, developed by the North Side Civic Development Council in Pittsburgh. In Washington, D.C., besides helping the Peoples Involvement Corporation, LISC has supplied financing both to the H Street CDC, which is developing a $23.5 million commercial project near Union Station, and to the Marshall Heights Development Organization, which bought and rehabilitated a fourteen-store shopping center.

Across the country, the LISC "experiment" so far has received mostly positive reviews. A two-year evaluation by a team of researchers from Harvard University's John F. Kennedy School of Government, looking closely at thirty-four LISC-funded groups and sixty-six projects, found LISC had been "highly successful" in developing a "new technology" for neighborhood development.

Any operation as significant as LISC arouses some criticism. It ranges from charges that LISC has not paid enough attention to building the capacity of its groups to complaints that it is overly "parental." Some contend LISC's focus — to be a bank — isn't "systems-changing" enough. Grogan acknowledges some problems, including instances of inadequate follow-up: "LISC began with a lot of fanfare in many cities, getting the attention of the right private-sector people, eliciting a good-to-spectacular level of involvement," he says. "Very frequently, that was the last time people at that level heard anything about LISC. In many cases, we've not been attentive enough to opportunities to re-enthuse people by placing the results of their involvement before them."

As 1986 drew to a close, LISC announced the creation of yet another financing innovation, a new secondary market for CDC loans, to be called the Local Initiatives Managed Assets Corporation (LIMAC). Capitalized with $10 million contributed by four large insurance companies and the Ford and MacArthur foundations, LIMAC will buy up loans made to CDCs by LISC and other financiers, then resell them. The goal is to raise fresh capital to invest in new CDC projects while giving the purchasers of the loans, many heretofore uninvolved in CDC financing, a low-risk way to assist community development without incurring the transaction costs and other expenses of lending directly to individual projects.

THE ENTERPRISE FOUNDATION

By 1986 this four-year-old national intermediary had supplied more than $7 million in grants and loans, not to mention substantial technical assistance, to sixty community-based organizations in twenty-six cities. Enterprise is the brainchild of James W. Rouse, the multimillionaire real estate developer, renowned for shopping centers (he built the first enclosed mall in America in 1958), for Columbia, Md. (the patch of farm land that Rouse turned into a thriving community of 60,000), and most of all, for the numerous festival marketplaces that are helping to anchor the revival of decayed waterfronts and downtowns from Boston to Milwaukee.

After stepping down as chief executive officer of the Rouse Company in 1979, Rouse established the Enterprise Foundation to focus on the housing needs of the very poorest Americans — the more than 13 million families with annual incomes below $10,000. Headquartered in Columbia, Md., the Enterprise Foundation network now extends from Boston, Baltimore, and Philadelphia to Chicago, Dallas, Denver, and Oakland.

Like LISC, Enterprise can claim more than 100 foundation and corporate sponsors — including CIGNA, Metropolitan Life, Atlantic Richfield, Alcoa, CBS, Merrill Lynch, PPG Industries, Standard Oil, the Ford Foundation, and the Rouse Company itself, which contributed over $1 million. But the plan is for Enterprise eventually to derive most of its revenues from its own for-profit subsidiary, the Enterprise Development Co., which has continued to build the more familiar Rouse downtown projects — among them Waterside Mall in Norfolk, Portside in Toledo, and Richmond's Sixth Street Marketplace.

Rouse's personal involvement in the housing arena spans more than half a century, beginning with a job at age 19 in the New Deal's Federal Housing Administration. Over the next four decades, he served on numerous task forces and commissions, helping to write the 1954 Federal Housing Act (some credit him with coining the term "urban renewal"). His wife Patricia, an officer in the Enterprise Foundation, was for five years a housing commissioner in Norfolk.

Rouse credits the congregants of the Church of the Savior in Washington, D.C., as his inspiration for establishing the Enterprise Foundation. In 1973 they approached him for assistance in rehabilitating two dilapidated apartment buildings for low-income residents of the city's fast-gentrifying Adams Morgan neighborhood. Rouse first tried to steer them to government programs, but finally, impressed with their commitment and determination, he agreed to personally finance the buildings' $625,000 purchase price.

Rouse recalls the first visit to "his" apartments: "The stench was so terrible I gagged. Garbage and rubbish were piled in the stairwells and elevator shaft. There was no front door and the mailboxes had been ripped out. There were 947 housing-code violations. It was just a pest hole — but fully occupied."

To do the work, the congregants formed Jubilee Housing, which mobilized neighborhood residents to contribute some 50,000 hours of "sweat equity." Jubilee subsequently became the flagship of the Enterprise Foundation network. It acquired eight buildings and established a pre-school, a learning center for youthful parents, a shelter and infirmary for the homeless, the Columbia Road Health Services clinic, which serves more than 25,000 patients annually, and Jubilee-Jobs, a highly successful job-placement service that has been replicated in ten cities.

"Jubilee is one of the best examples of comprehensive neighborhood development in our network," says Edward Quinn, president of the Enterprise Foundation. "But we learned right away you can't replicate Jubilee or any model. We consider each city unique, and work with what we find there."

Once groups become part of the Enterprise network, the relationship

A dry cleaning store at the Plaza de Santa Fe Shopping Center in West Denver. The center was developed by NEWSED Community Development Corporation.

continues even after a particular project is finished. The whole network convenes annually. "We don't try to change the priorities of our groups, but rather to help them improve their methods," says F. Barton Harvey, the Wall Street investment banker Rouse recruited to be his deputy chairman. "Our object," Harvey says, "is to find the pieces out there and incorporate them into a rational whole."

One division of the foundation, the Enterprise Social Investment Corporation, develops sources of financing for low-income housing. Another division, the Rehabilitation Work Group, seeks ways to cut rehab costs, sometimes succeeding by as much as 40 percent. Rouse credits the Cleveland Housing Network with originating many of the new techniques. He explains: "We conserve everything that is sound and usable — bathroom fixtures, kitchen cabinets, windows, doors, walls, and partitions." The groups are told to avoid architects and are trained to be their own contractors. The foundation provides on-site training, publishes a monthly newsletter *(Cost Cuts)* and a 500-page manual on how to renovate more cheaply. It offers prizes for the best cost-cutting ideas, and develops computer software to produce quick, reliable rehab specifications, estimates, bid packages, and job-cost reports. The foundation also works with major producers of modular, factory-built homes to help supply more low-cost housing, and has pioneered a system of warehousing bulk purchases, private builders' salvaged goods, and donated building materials for use by its nonprofits.

Like Jubilee and Bethel New Life, many of the groups in the Enterprise Foundation network reflect substantial ecumenical involvement. For instance, Hope Communities, a CDC in Denver, grew out of a local church consortium that used Jubilee as its model. Since 1980 Hope has rehabilitated fifty-three housing units, with thirty more in the works, in Denver's Five Points, a predominantly black neighborhood near downtown, where one in four families depends on Aid to Families with Dependent Children and another 36 percent are elderly Social Security recipients. Hope Communities sponsors a "benevolent" loan fund, a lease-purchase program for low-income renters, food clubs, community gardens, block captains, and a mother-to-mother friendship club that matches Five Points women with women from the suburbs.

The Enterprise Foundation launched its most ambitious experiment in Chattanooga in 1985. Its goal: to make *all* the city's housing "fit and livable" within a decade. Working hand-in-hand with city officials, local business leaders, and Chattanooga Venture, a nonprofit citizens' organization, Enterprise had by 1987 targeted 14,000 units in need of renovation and devised a business plan for financing. Projected cost: $200 million. Despite the enthusiasm with which the project was greeted in Chattanooga, it was experimental, Rouse acknowledges. "The answers on how to do this in ten years do not now exist," he says, but adds: "I've always had the conviction that if cities will take on the whole job, it's a lot easier than doing part. If we can get this program advancing on schedule, even if we don't have all the work completed in ten years, we will have built a structure that will change housing for the poor in America. It will be a lighthouse for other cities to follow."

DEVELOPMENT TRAINING INSTITUTE (DTI)

Since 1982 more than 150 CDC directors and senior development managers from across the nation have graduated from what DTI President Joseph McNeely calls "the Berlitz School of community development." This intensive one-year training program teaches the fine art of business and real estate development, finance, organization and management, and strategic planning at the neighborhood level. Participants begin the course with two weeks of highly structured, all-day workshops. Then they go back to their jobs, returning to DTI every four months for one week of workshops. In between, they are expected to apply what they have learned to their own projects, assisted by individually tailored assignments and on-site visits from DTI staff.

"We're looking for people who are already engaged in development, not groups thinking about that possibility," McNeely explains. "This is a functional language. You've got to go use it, or you'll lose it." The best students, McNeely reports, are those who come to DTI after they have a project or two under their belt. "This becomes a way for them to understand the process they went through and how to apply it over and over again," he says.

As one key component of the training, each participant develops a "mentor" relationship with an important private business leader or developer in his or her city. Equally important, McNeely stresses, is DTI's goal of creating a long-range network, "a knowledge institute" of community-based developers. Alumni meet regularly. "We work hard at building a collaborative learning community that will last beyond the internship," McNeely says. "One of the most exciting things is that now we have 150 people who all use the same vocabulary and have the same conceptual framework. What a power that is."

DTI's partner in the New York City area is Pratt Institute's Center for Community and Environmental Development, which cooperated with McNeely in developing the national training model. By early 1987 the Pratt training program, funded through the Revson Foundation, had turned out fifty-five graduates in the New York-New Jersey-Connecticut region.

For PIC's Director Andree Gandy, the DTI network has been a valuable source of support. "People call me all the time, asking about this project or that," she says. "And I don't feel as lonely when I can phone someone and say, 'Boy is this a mess.'" Another DTI graduate, Lynette Jung Lee, director of East Bay Asian Local Development Corp., says: "Many of us really do feel a special close bond to each other."

Providing high-caliber training isn't cheap. DTI has raised funds from more than seventy corporations and foundations, mostly in cities that send interns to DTI for training (each intern is expected to help raise his or her tuition). But support has also come from major national organizations, including the Rockefeller Brothers Fund, Levi-Strauss, the Ford and Charles S. Mott foundations, and the federal Economic Development Administration. In conjunction with the Council on Foundations, DTI also sponsors an annual program for funders to acquaint them with CDC activities.

The DTI program receives generally excellent reviews. "A corporate leader in Pittsburgh told me that our program has changed the dynamic of leadership in his city," McNeely says. "Five years ago, all of the policy initiatives toward neighborhood development were coming from a small cadre of private business and public leaders. Now he tells me that our graduates are the ones who lead the process and are genuinely respected."

McNeely, a lawyer with a master's degree in psychology, headed a Baltimore CDC in the 1970s before being tapped by Geno Baroni, assistant secretary of the Department of Housing and Urban Development, to head HUD's Office of Neighborhood Development. McNeely believes that CDC leadership and professional skills are growing all the time. But he adds: "One thing we've learned over the years is that good organizations do not exist everywhere. The vital principle is a committed, respected, neighborhood leadership base. There is little that outsiders — the federal government, philanthropies — can do to create that base. But where it exists, we should support the hell out of it."

OTHER INTERMEDIARIES

One can count perhaps a hundred organizations at the national, regional, or local levels (and likely there are even more) that provide vital assistance to community-based development. Here's a sampling:

In financing, there is the National Cooperative Bank and its risk-capital branch, the NCB Development Corporation. Chartered by the U.S. Congress in 1978 and converted to private ownership in 1982, this intermediary provides equity capital, loans, and "business-planning advances" to commercial and housing cooperatives, including some CDCs. Another financial intermediary, one of the country's oldest, is the Cooperative Assistance Fund, a "social investment" fund begun in 1968 by eight foundations and corporations; it has supported community development to the tune of more than $6 million. The National Trust for Historic Preservation, through its Inner City Ventures Fund, has provided $2.6 million in loans and grants to community-based developers that preserve historic housing for low-income residents. It has also funded some commercial development.

Like LISC and the Enterprise Foundation, some intermediaries are working to develop new financing tools for CDCs. One promising new tool is the "community loan fund," which by 1987 had blossomed in more than two dozen cities. The model fund was started in 1979 by the Institute for Community Economics (ICE) in Greenfield, Mass., which has worked aggressively to spread the model nationwide. Typically, the funds are capitalized by "socially responsible" investors, primarily individuals, but also religious groups, corporations, and foundations. The depositors are paid a return, usually — though not always — at rates somewhat below those offered by such traditional investment vehicles as savings accounts, money markets, mutual funds, or certificates of deposit. The money in the funds is then loaned at attractive rates to community development projects.

By 1987 a national network of community loan funds had been established. All told, its members had raised more than $31 million for community development projects and had made some 11,000 loans. Most of the loan funds are small, averaging around $200,000. But ICE's Revolving Loan Fund has topped the $4 million mark, financed by more than 185 investors, including, says Chuck Matthei, ICE director, "wealthy people and people of very modest means, older people whose life savings are invested, and children whose college trust funds have been invested by their parents." Religious organizations, banks, investment firms, and foundations have also placed funds in ICE's community loan fund.

For legal advice, CDCs can turn to the National Economic Development and Law Center in Berkeley, Calif.; the National Housing Law Project, also in Berkeley; or the Council of New York Law Associates. For academic and research support, there is Cleveland State University's College of Urban Affairs; the Center for Community Development and Design at the University of Colorado at Denver; the master's program in community economic development at New Hampshire College in Manchester, N.H.; the New School for Social Research in New York City; the Woodstock Institute in Chicago; and Pratt Institute in Brooklyn, N.Y.

For policy-making and tactical assistance, there are many organizations, some with their own local networks. Among the most active are the Center for Community Change and the National Center for Policy Alternatives, both in Washington, D.C.; the Association of Communities Organized for Reform Now (ACORN), which is active in several cities across the United States; and the National Training and Information Center, the potent

Chicago-based organization led by Gale Cincotta. Other Washington, D.C.-based national intermediaries include the Corporation for Enterprise Development; the National Center for Neighborhood Enterprise; and the National Council of La Raza.

Numerous groups assist in the housing arena, including Low Income Housing Information Services, a technical assistance organization; the National Mutual Housing Network; the Housing Assistance Council, promoter and financier of rural housing since the 1960s; the California-based Trust for Public Lands; and Habitat for Humanity, which concentrates on housing for the very poorest Americans.

A major player in the housing field is the congressionally chartered Neighborhood Reinvestment Corporation and its huge network of Neighborhood Housing Services (NHS) partnerships across the United States, now numbering more than 130 groups in 210 neighborhoods. Each NHS is locally initiated and funded, and governed by boards of residents, business leaders, and government representatives. Their main focus is on financing home purchases for residents of lower-income neighborhoods. By 1986 the NHS network had brokered more than 11,000 loans, worth over $110 million. A range of technical assistance and other services is also provided, including a secondary market that has recycled more than $25 million worth of NHS loans. NHS groups are not technically CDCs, though their missions often overlap with CDC aims.

CDCs have their own national membership organization – the National Congress for Community Economic Development. So, too, do community development assistance providers – the National Neighborhood Coalition. Both groups are based in Washington, D.C.

Quite a few organizations with wide-ranging agendas have special programs to assist CDCs. One is the National Urban Coalition. Its spin-off nonprofit, the Community Information Exchange, offers CDCs technical assistance and a computerized data base of community-based development ventures. The National Civic League's "CIVITEX" system offers a more broadly defined data base on locally based initiatives and partnerships.

Some of the most vital support networks for CDCs exist at the city and metropolitan level, where they have expanded rapidly in the 1980s. They provide CDCs with links to powerful financial institutions, political leaders, and philanthropies. They also help link CDCs working in different neighborhoods. Among cities, Chicago may have the broadest array of local community development intermediaries. Groups include the Chicago Rehab Network, the Chicago Equity Fund, the Chicago Association of Neighborhood Development Organizations, and the Community Workshop on Economic Development. Elsewhere, prominent local intermediaries include the Piton Foundation in Denver, the Urban Affairs Partnership in

Philadelphia, the Cleveland Housing Network, Greater Boston Community Development, and the Neighborhood Fund in Pittsburgh.

It seems as if each year of the 1980s has brought stronger backing and more sophisticated networks to help CDCs reach their full potential. Yet, as the realistic supporters of the movement stress, the surface has barely been scratched — in neighborhoods covered, in investments made, in financial and corporate assistance mobilized, in public recognition of the central role community development could play in bringing the opportunities of the American economic system to peoples and neighborhoods long excluded.

A sign of hope in the South Bronx is this community garden. Other signs: rising property values, new businesses, a growing sense of community pride.

Gaining Ground

The South Bronx, 1986. A sunny Halloween afternoon. Kids are trooping home from school, sporting their costumes. Pumpkins, black cats, skeletons hang in doors and windows. At a renovated tenement, a security guard stands nonchalantly by the entrance; a Hispanic mother and her children lean out of their second-floor apartment window to chat with visitors. Across the street, behind him the hulk of one of the few torched buildings still standing, an old man shows off his plot in the carefully fenced-in community garden. "Here are my squash, my pumpkins, my peppers — they're very hot," he says.

Statistics confirm a community on the upswing: property values and commercial rents rising, crime declining, new businesses moving in. Thousands of units of new and rehabilitated housing have risen from the ashes; a few choice blocks of historic homes brace for gentrification. The fields of rubble have been covered with grass. Many streets have been repaved, many have new sidewalks and lighting. On Kelly Street, there's a new $7 million municipal park, the first built in decades. On infamous Charlotte Street, where Presidents Carter and Reagan came to view the rubble, one is now shocked to discover suburban-style ranch houses, complete with pretty lawns and portable swimming pools; one house has a van in front and a satellite dish.

No one pretends the South Bronx has purged all its social pathologies. Its schools are plagued by some of New York's lowest test scores and highest high school dropout rates. Drugs are still sold openly on some streets. A huge portion of the population remains on welfare. Southern Boulevard, lined with little shops, pulses with activity, but virtually all the profits go to outside owners. Some of the CDCs that began the rebirth, including Megan Charlop's People's Development Corporation have gone out of existence or changed their focus. (PDC has left housing development and now lacks anything resembling its leadership role of the 1970s. But it does continue, under a city contract, to manage housing units, and runs weatherization, adult education, and social service programs. Megan Charlop's life has taken her into other professional fields.)

What's important to note is that the seed of indigenous economic development has been planted on these barren fields. At East 134th and Walnut, there's a fully occupied "business incubator" for fledgling entrepreneurs. And for a major source of new jobs, there is the new Bathgate Industrial Park, replacing rubble-strewn lots with single-story plants built by the city government and the Port Authority of New York and New Jersey. Typical tenants: a printing plant and a ladies' shoulder-pad maker — both having fled crowded and expensive Manhattan. A pharmaceutical firm. An art restoration guild. A computer equipment company begun by three young South Bronx Puerto Ricans. And the most famous of all: GLIE Farms and its hydroponic greenhouse, fast becoming the premier producer of fresh herbs for eastern America.

Is the palpable recovery a work of government? In one sense, yes. Millions of dollars have flowed from government coffers to repair this most grievously wounded city neighborhood in American history — first federal money in the late 1970s, increasingly city and state funds in the 1980s.

But the true heroes of the South Bronx's rebirth do not sit in distant legislatures or city hall. They are the South Bronx's own people: leaders of churches, neighborhood groups, block clubs, CDCs. A prime example: the South East Bronx Community Organization of Father Louis Gigante, the priest from St. Athanasius Church who has sparked rehabilitation of a phenomenal 2,300 units of apartment housing in the Hunts Point section. So profound is his impact that some now call the neighborhood "Gigante Land."

In fact, there is a new demarcation across the South Bronx's neighborhoods. Chunks of territory once staked out by rival gangs of knife- and gun-wielding youth have been rechristened with the names of community development organizations. The Banana Kelly Community Improvement Association. The Mid Bronx Desperadoes (managing the new housing at Charlotte Street). The NW Bronx Community Clergy Coalition. BUILD. Cumulatively, they represent a dynamic force for economic regeneration.

In 1977 the South Bronx symbolized death. In 1987 it mirrors life.